Albert S. Bolles

Chapters in Political Economy

Albert S. Bolles

Chapters in Political Economy

ISBN/EAN: 9783337241971

Printed in Europe, USA, Canada, Australia, Japan

Cover: Foto ©Suzi / pixelio.de

More available books at **www.hansebooks.com**

CHAPTERS IN

POLITICAL ECONOMY.

BY

ALBERT S. BOLLES.

NEW YORK:
D. APPLETON & COMPANY,
549 AND 551 BROADWAY.
1874.

ENTERED, according to Act of Congress, in the year 1874, by
D. APPLETON & COMPANY,
In the Office of the Librarian of Congress at Washington.

TO

ALBERT P. STURTEVANT, Esq.

THIS VOLUME IS DEDICATED

AS A TOKEN OF

THE AUTHOR'S AFFECTIONATE REGARD.

PREFACE.

The chapters embraced in this work treat of the leading economic questions which are rife in our country. Although most of the chapters have appeared in magazines during the past two years, yet a unity will be found pervading the work. An attempt has been made to handle the questions in a thorough manner, to dig down for principles which are fundamental, though the author was conscious that, in so doing, the work would lose something of its interest to those who only seek to glide over the surface of things. If ever the questions of labor, money, exchange, taxation, and the like, are to receive a permanent settlement, they must be traced back into the region where prejudice and feeling do not enter, however dry and uninviting may be the investigation.

Norwich, Conn., September, 1874.

CONTENTS.

	PAGE.
I.—THE FIELD AND IMPORTANCE OF POLITICAL ECONOMY,	1
II.—THE PAYMENT OF LABOR,	15
III.—ON THE INCREASE OF WAGES,	28
IV.—EFFECT OF MACHINERY ON LABOR,	41
V.—ON THE MEANING AND CAUSES OF VALUE,	48
VI.—A MEASURE OF VALUE,	73
VII.—MONEY AND ITS USES,	81
VIII.—DECLINE IN THE VALUE OF GOLD AND SILVER,	101
IX.—THE MONEY OF THE FUTURE,	113
X.—THE GOOD AND EVIL OF BANKING,	117
XI.—THE FINANCIAL PANIC OF 1873,	140
XII.—THE RELATION OF BANKS TO SPECULATORS,	149
XIII.—THE INFLUENCE OF CREDIT ON PRICES,	166
XIV.—ON LEGAL INTERFERENCE WITH THE LOAN OF MONEY, PAYMENT OF LABOR, AND CONTRACTS OF CORPORATIONS,	170
XV.—THE ADVANTAGES OF EXCHANGE,	190
XVI.—TAXATION,	200

I.

THE FIELD AND IMPORTANCE OF POLITICAL ECONOMY.

In *The Principles of Economical Philosophy*,* MACLEOD has given an elaborate criticism upon several definitions of political economy, and then offered one himself which, in his opinion, "appears to state clearly and distinctly the nature and extent of the science, and to be free from the ambiguities connected with the words wealth and value." At the risk of being ambiguous, we shall not give a definition so precise, because a commoner one can be more easily understood. According to an old and well-received definition, the principles of political economy relate to the production, distribution, exchange, and consumption of wealth. No higher origin is claimed for these principles than an enlightened self-interest. They are such as every man entertains having regard solely for his own interests from the most enlightened point of view.

Although without moral foundation, these principles yield the same results in the production, distribution, exchange, and consumption of wealth, as obedience to a perfect moral code. Wherever economic and moral science touch, the principles of human

* P. 122, 2d ed.

conduct prescribed by each are seen to be the same.* The remark of Dr. WAYLAND is perfectly true, that "the principles of political economy are so clearly analogous to those of moral philosophy, that almost every question in the one may be argued on grounds belonging to the other."†

For example, moral science condemns laws made in restraint of trade.‡ It teaches that every man has the right to traffic where he pleases, unfettered by State lines. The primary object of enacting such laws is to enrich the few at the expense of the many. The protectionist urges their enactment for the public good, or for some reason beyond his own aggrandizement; the history of legislation clearly shows that the prime object of all protective laws is to benefit particular individuals, or a class, and not all. Of course, moral science condemns such legislation.

They are condemned by political economy also, which looks at them with the sharp eye of enlightened selfishness. It sees that if the public good is the object of protection, everything must be protected conducive to that end; and if this doctrine be admitted, protective laws will be enacted so generally as to afford protection to nothing. If the principle is not to receive a logical and just application, and merely that a few things most needed by the public are to be protected, their increased cost to the consumer will result in his protecting himself by charging more for whatever he sells, so that, after a time, the effect of protective laws is completely neutralized.

Moral science, then, condemns legal protection because it is wrong; economic science because it is impossible to get protection by operation of law. The conduct of people in either case is the

* PERRY'S *El. of Polit. Econ.*, p. 37, 5th ed.
† Pref. *El. of Polit. Econ.*, p. 4, 4th ed.
‡ For an elucidation of the operation of protective laws, see chap. 15th.

same, only it is impelled by different motives in one case than in the other.

As this position will hardly be assailed by any one—that the principles of economic and moral science yield the same results—is it not better to transfer the principles of political economy from a selfish to a moral basis? We favor this transfer for four reasons.

First, more persons will be drawn to the study of economic principles. Now, it is said, they are cold and bloodless, and tend to increase human selfishness. If made a portion of the truths of moral science, this objection to them will disappear.

Secondly, in the classification of knowledge, it will be easier to find an appropriate place for political economy. Instead of being a piece of knowledge standing apart by itself, it will form a subdivision of moral science. Political economy in that case would constitute that part of moral science relating to the production, distribution, exchange, and consumption of wealth.

Thirdly, after deriving the principles from a moral source, they can be enforced by showing their harmony with enlightened self-interest. Thus the combined power of morality and selfishness can be used to sustain these principles by founding them upon a moral basis. We have previously seen in the example of protective legislation, how the selfish mind, cold, clear, and enlightened, supplements and enforces the transparent conclusions of morality. Moral science condemns such laws because they are wrong; economic science because they are at war with self-interest and have only a nominal, and not a real, existence after a period.*

Fourthly, political economy is properly a subdivision of moral science, because the will operates in every transaction with which

* The insufficiency of enlightened self-interest as a competent basis for economic science has been ably discussed by FREDERIC HARRISON in the *Fort. Rev.*, vol. 1, p. 256.

economic science is concerned. This faculty exercises only moral functions. If the principles of political economy were immutable, if the will were a stranger in their production, if no moral quality adhered to them, political economy would be entitled to a seat among the exact sciences. But these principles are not fixed, because the human will is an element determining what they are. The rules which have guided men in the past respecting the acquisition or disposition of their wealth, are only hypotheses in respect to what they will do in the future. Quite absurd is the claim that economic principles are absolutely fixed, and therefore purely scientific principles. Having no place in exact literature, and the will being a part of the machinery by which economic principles are created, they ought to be relegated to the domain of moral science.*

If the principles of political economy are transferred from a selfish to a moral basis, the method of searching for them is not changed. Economic principles are still the fruit of induction. And it is worthy of note how extensively employed is the inductive method in political economy. ADAM SMITH, it is true, did not write an inductive treatise. His *Wealth of Nations* is a great landmark in the history of thought, but its success is due to the fact that he put ten years of patient labor upon the work, combining in the happiest manner a philosophic insight with a knowledge of practical life, deducing therefrom principles which have found universal acceptance. It is easier to dream and speculate than to burrow amid a great mass of facts; yet, as the gold in the

---

* JEVONS, in his *Theory of Polit. Econ.*, has united moral and economic science, making pleasure the end, and declaring that "the object of economy is to maximise happiness by purchasing pleasure, as it were, at the lowest cost of pain" (p. 27). As JEVONS is a utilitarian, of course pleasure is the highest end for man according to his philosophy, though he gives a wider interpretation to the term than his master, BENTHAM, whom he so much admires. See pp. 27-32.

earth can be found only by toilsome mining, so the gold of economic truth is hid in great masses of facts which must be dug over to find it. Never did finer logicians or acuter reasoners exist than the schoolmen; never did a class of men commit greater mistakes. These followed from wrong premises. Political economy has followed too much a similar method. This is one reason why it has failed to convert men. It has been too speculative.* The change of method among economists in this respect is remarkable. Fifty years since, THOMAS TOOKE applied the inductive method in his *History of Prices* with enduring success. Later, RICHARD JONES applied it to the subject of Rent; similarly, EDWIN CHADWICK in his investigations into the questions of Factory and Infantile Labor, and Sanitary and Poor-Law Legislation. In 1867, ROGERS published his work upon the *Agricultural Prices and Wages in England during the Twelfth and Thirteenth Centuries*, a monument of patient investigation, a work which gave a new rendering of the social and economic history of ENGLAND for the period it covered, "enabling us to see," says NEWMARCH,† "in detail, how far-reaching and potent were wages, prices, and pestilences in modifying from top to bottom the coherence of the English polity, and the power of our sovereign lord the king, under the early Plantagenets."

Other economic works might be spoken of, prepared in a similar way, DUDLEY BAXTER's books upon *National Income*, and *Taxation of the United Kingdom*, and LEONI LEVI's *History of British Commerce*, are examples. As for FRANCE, she has been noted for her economists who have burrowed and lived among the facts.

---

* "Half, and more than half, of the fallacies into which persons who have handled this subject have fallen, are the direct outcome of purely abstract speculation." ROGERS in preface to his edition of *Smith's Wealth of Nations*, p. 41.

† Address before the British Social Science Association, 1871.

CHEVALIER, in all his works, has kept close to the inductive method. So has M. DE LAVERGNE when treating upon the moral economy of his own and other countries. M. LEVASSEUR and M. LE PLAY have considered the claims of the working classes of FRANCE in a similar manner. The same may be said of M. JULES SIMON.

Of the political economists in our own country following this method, not so much can be said. The most prominent example who has addressed himself to the mastery of facts as the foundation of his subsequent reasonings, is DAVID A. WELLS. In his reports to the National Government and to the State of NEW YORK, and in other papers, he has adhered rigidly to the inductive method. For many years pursuing physical science, he has employed its methods in finding out the principles of political economy. His results have, in some instances, been as unexpected to himself as they were startling to the public. They are none the less true, however, or less likely of being accepted in the end. The National and State Governments are learning the value of this method, for they are appointing commissions and requiring investigation and reports upon many subjects lying in the province of political economy. Never was a more inviting field of investigation open to the student of economic science than our own country, nor one where patient, honest investigation was more needed. The facts are lying around in the greatest profusion, while the honest and accurate gatherers are few.

Although the true principles of political economy are ascertained by induction, and all others are only guessed, yet none are hard, fixed laws that never change in their occurrence, like the movements of the sun. On the other hand, the element of human freedom, as we have previously remarked, enters into their composition, preventing us from determining their absolute truth, as we can the laws of physical science. MACLEOD, in his *Principles of Economical Philosophy*,* has labored industriously, and with great ability, to bring economic science within the domain of physical science, but we cannot regard his attempt as successful. COMTE and JOHN STUART MILL have comprehended the nature of economic principles more perfectly. They admit the play of the human will; hence the Frenchman was consistent in rejecting political economy from his scheme of positive philosophy. One of his disciples,† in vindicating his master, has very well said: "So far as physical conditions go, and up to a point where moral conditions begin, strict scientific laws can be established. . . Directly the data of the study become affected by moral conditions, the conclusions of the economist as such cease to be scientific laws, and are only hypotheses." For this reason, therefore, political economy can never become an exact science. However far we may carry our inductions, a large element of variation must be allowed for the action of the will. As the land surveyor can never determine with exactness surface and direction on account of variation of the needle, so the economist can never discover by the most patient study of facts, any unalterable laws of economic science, because of the infinite variations in the will of men. The farthest he can go is to ascertain how men have acted under former conditions, and form the hypothesis that, under like conditions, similar actions will be produced.‡

As the principles of political economy are ascertained by induc-

---

* Chap. 1. † FREDERIC HARRISON, *Fort. Review*, vol. 1, p. 369.

‡ DAVID SYME has declared that the "inductive method is alone applicable to the investigation of economic science, and that we shall never be able to make any solid progress so long as we continue to follow the A PRIORI method." *West. Rev.*, vol. 95, p. 100. On same subject, see Prof. CAIRNES' *Character and Logical Method of Polit. Econ.*, Lec. 11.

tion, any one capable of making an induction can find them out. A knowledge of economic principles involved in a particular pursuit is not necessarily limited to those engaged in that business. The sole advantage one man has over another of equal ability is in a knowledge of facts, out of which inductions spring.

Thus the charge, that only business men, practical men, can understand the principles of political economy, is conclusively refuted. The charge contains this basis of truth and no more—that business men often know more facts concerning their business than outsiders; hence they are more capable of forming correct conclusions.

The history of political economy attests the truth of this assertion. For, who are the most successful cultivators of the science? Who have wrought out those principles which most persons are willing to admit as true and of great importance? Are they the discovery of practical men? By no means. The great lights in economic science, from the day of ADAM SMITH to this, have not been practical men.* Political economists have walked with the man of business, have gleaned from him all that he knew, and, not content with exhausting one storehouse of experience, have exhausted others, dug in rare and rich mines of which practical men had no knowledge perhaps, or no time or inclination to explore. As the reader of the description of a battle may acquire a more perfect knowledge of it than a participator therein, because, as an eye-witness, the latter knows only what happened immediately around him, so the political economist may acquire a wider knowledge of economic principles governing a particular business

---

* "In every country in which it has been successfully cultivated, most of the contributions to it of any value have been made by writers who were not of the business world, but surveyed its operations from a distance; men for whose opinions on business matters few merchants or manufacturers would have given five cents." *The Nation*, vol. 2, p. 146.

even, than a person who has given to it the attention of a lifetime.

A political economist can see economic principles more clearly because his view is not mystified by pecuniary interest. His judgments are unclouded by prejudice; undisturbed by the thought of gain or loss. We need not indulge in any platitudes as to the unconscious warpings of opinions and beliefs by interest and desire; the fact is common to all.

A conspicuous illustration of the eminent service sometimes rendered by the theoretical economist, is the creation of the National banking system. This was the work of the Rev. JOHN McVICKAR, Professor of Political Economy in Columbia College. In 1827, he wrote a letter to a member of the legislature of the State of NEW YORK, entitled *Hints on Banking*, in which he developed the system now in practice. This discovery excited the admiration of an eminent banker, JOHN E. WILLIAMS, President of the METROPOLITAN BANK of New York, who has remarked that "to a practical man of business—an every-day banker—it seems wonderful that a scholar, investigating questions in political economy, on purely scientific principles, should be able to see not only the practical workings of existing laws, and understand the indissoluble relations of money and trade, but should be also able to foresee and foretell what changes were necessary to produce the highest prosperity and secure the greatest safety to the community." *

Not infrequently the principles of political economy are declared to be mere theories. Some of them are nothing more. The difference, however, between theoretical principles, and those derived from experience, is clear enough. Scientists are continually mistaking principles for theories, regarding things as proved which are

* *Old and New Mag.*, vol. 8, p. 590.

not, but only asserted or believed. That theories are useless, as some contend, we deny. Nay, they are absolutely necessary; no man can conduct his business without them. "What is practice without theory," enquires an eminent French economist,* "but the employment of means without knowing how or why they act." To which the words of Prof. Price† may be added. "It is a mistake, though a very common one, to suppose that practical men, as they are called, are destitute of theory. The exact reverse of this statement is true. Practical men swarm with theories, none more so." Theories are well enough,‡ only they must be regarded as such; no harm is done to economic science in including both, if the separation of principle from theory be clearly made.

The flaw with some of the principles of political economy, like many of the inductions of science, is that they rest upon insufficient foundations. A few facts are gathered, and from them a principle is deduced, which, indeed, may be correct, yet which would give way to another principle, perhaps, were a wider induction made. Every result is produced by several causes, nevertheless we are constantly blundering by satisfying ourselves with finding a single cause, and so look no farther.

To some it may seem a waste of time and space to say anything concerning the importance of knowing the principles of political economy. Yet there are peculiar reasons for saying something on this point. The extraordinary prosperity that has visited our country has spread a kind of poetic haze over the whole machinery of society, and led us to regard all inquiry into its

---

* Say. *Treat. on Polit. Econ.*, Intro., p. 24, 4th Am. ed. † *Princ. of Currency*, p. 1.

‡ Sir William Hamilton says: "Theory is dependent on practice; practice must have preceded theory; for theory being a generalization of the principles on which practice proceeds, these must originally have been taken out of, or abstracted from, practice." *Lecture on Met.*, p. 120, Am. ed.

working as an idle speculation. Before the enactment of the great tragedy between the North and South, there were but few questions relating to the administration of the government involving the application of any principles of political economy. The great debates in Congress were upon constitutional law, internal improvements, slavery, and like questions. With the breaking out of war, these questions passed away. The country had gone through the formative period of finding out the meaning and scope of the organic law. Congress was confronted with economic questions. With these it was ill prepared to deal. It had only the scantiest knowledge of them, except the question of taxing importations. The *Congressional Globe* is the enduring monument of the ignorance displayed by members of congress upon questions involving economic principles.*

To what new economic conditions did the war give rise? It created a great debt, the interest and principal of which must be provided for and paid. A national currency and system of banking have been created. How our country blundered in raising money to maintain the war, and spent it; how the strife might have been carried on and the debt been less than half it is, are mistakes which we shall not recall.

Unquestionably our country has suffered most fearfully from an ignorance of, or failure to apply, some of the most familiar principles of political economy. One of its most distinguished teachers,

---

* We shall give a couple of fair specimens. "All governments fix the value of gold and silver; and without their government stamp gold and silver would be a simple commodity, like other things having intrinsic value. Some governments fix the value of coin higher, and some lower; just as each for itself chooses to determine."—E. G. SPAULDING: *speech on Demand-Note Bill, January 28, 1862.*

"'This currency," referring to demand notes or legal tenders, "can be converted in such a manner as to yield six per cent interest on its par value; it can never greatly depreciate, because the moment the capitalist holding it sees any evidence of its depreciation, he will convert it into the bonds bearing interest, giving him a permanent income. Thus it secures itself against over-circulation."—*Speech of* SAMUEL HOOPER *on same subject.*

AMASA WALKER, clearly set forth in a congressional speech, during the early part of the war, how it might be carried on at less than half the expense which Congress was likely to incur, by sticking to specie payments, instead of abandoning them for an irredeemable paper currency. His words, deemed foolish then, have long since borne evidence of their wisdom and truth. The issue of an irredeemable currency, so pointedly condemned by him and other economists, has wrought a thousand curses to our country, from which we are suffering to-day and are to suffer for years to come.

Letting the past go, many of our politicians do not yet understand the principles of political economy, the application of which are needed to settle questions confronting the nation. For example, there are questions of taxation both upon imports and property at home. The principles which should govern in these matters, some of our politicians are as ignorant of as the grandest truths in astronomy. The National banking system, the currency, free banking, specie payments, redemption of legal-tender notes—are all subjects within the domain of political economy, whose principles must be mastered if these matters are to receive a rational settlement. The views entertained upon these questions, the nonsense and ignorance displayed by Congress when grappling with them, would be laughable were the results not so sad and so disastrous to the people.

Every session of Congress discloses its inability to grapple with economic questions.* When matters of foreign policy are discussed,

---

* Perhaps our congressmen may profit by learning what BURKE thought of political economy: "If I had not deemed it of some value, I should not have made political economy an object of my humble studies from my very early youth to near the end of my service in Parliament, even before (at least to any knowledge of mine) it had employed the thoughts of speculative men in other parts of EUROPE. At that time it was still in its infancy in ENGLAND, where, in the last century, it had its origin. Great and learned men thought my studies were not wholly

or treatment of the Indians, or internal improvements, or, in the olden time, when dealing with slavery, a knowledge and mastery of the several subjects is evinced, although not all reached similar conclusions. This cannot be said of the senators and representatives in Congress in respect to economic questions, excepting a member who appears occasionally, for a brief season, within the national halls.

It is desirable, therefore, for every person proposing to serve his country in a public capacity to understand the principles of political economy, for they apply to the most important questions of national legislation.* No one will dispute how the character of national legislation has been changed by the war, and that financial measures and taxation are the most conspicuous questions upon which Congress legislates.

Again, the principles of political economy are growing in importance to the individual in his business relations. Consider the relations of capital and labor. How this question looms up before the whole world. It is one of the mightiest questions of the age. It has assumed a magnitude surpassed by no other. It is convulsing the business of manufacturing and other pursuits. For years and years this question will hang like a mighty cloud over the people. Is it not desirable to find out all that can be known concerning the relation of the capitalist and laborer? Yet who has investigated this question most profoundly? The political economist. The question lies within the domain of economic

thrown away, and deigned to communicate with me now and then on some particulars of their immortal works. Something of these studies may appear incidentally in some of the earliest things I published. The House has been witness to their effect, and has profited of them, more or less, for above eight-and-twenty years."—*Letter to a Noble Lord on the attacks upon his pension;* BURKE'S *works, vol.* 5, *p.* 192.

* Said COBDEN to the House of Commons, when addressing them on the corn laws: "It may be material for you to get right notions of political economy; questions of that kind will form a great part of the world's legislation for a long time to come."—*Speeches, vol.* 1, *p.* 384.

science. And it has been patiently and thoroughly investigated by the economist in all its phases.*

The same is true of other questions. Take the question of restrictive laws upon foreign importations, for example. Shall the policy of the government be continued? Is it for the advantage of any one; if so, whom? Are the laboring classes benefited by it? Is the National banking system a good one? Do we need more currency? These, and a host of similar questions, fall within the range of political economy, and have been more carefully investigated by economists than by empirics, who, possessing a little knowledge and having achieved fortunes, find it hard to believe that any one has anything to tell them upon trade, finance or commerce.†

For these special reasons, the principles of political economy have a value to the statesman and man of business hitherto unknown or denied.‡ It is gratifying to know that a knowledge of these principles is rapidly widening. The issuing of eleven editions of Prof. PERRY's *Elements of Political Economy* within so short a period, is proof that the people are awaking out of sleep and coming to believe that ignorance of the principles of political economy—which has cost us so much as a nation and as individuals—is not bliss pure and unalloyed. A little wisdom is to be preferred, and the streaks of light beginning to be seen in Congress we trust will grow in power and magnitude until that body possesses the knowledge necessary to discuss and settle wisely the great economic questions which involve the prosperity and happiness of the republic.

---

* If the remark of COBDEN be true—that "the principles of political economy have elevated the working class above the place they ever filled before"—should they not seek to master these principles?—*Speeches*. vol. 2, p. 373.

† The advantages to be derived by the Christian ministry from the study of political economy are admirably stated by Prof. BOARDMAN in the *Bib. Sacra*, vol. 23, p. 73.

‡ The reasons why political economy has not been cultivated in AMERICA, are concisely given in *The Nation*, vol. 2, p. 255.

II.

THE PAYMENT OF LABOR.

This question has attracted more attention in EUROPE, especially in ENGLAND, than here; for there laborers have been paid less and have suffered more, and they have oftener resorted to strikes and other rude methods to increase their wages. Yet the wave of discontent has reached our shore, and is breaking, with more or less fury, over every part of the land. Not a more important question in political economy calls for settlement; not one is likely to give rise to graver difficulties and greater suffering before a settlement is reached.

The contest between capitalist and laborer is a contest between present and accumulated labor. Capital is labor saved, nothing more.* The contest is between him who has saved his labor, or inherited it, and him who has less. It is a contest of the laborer with the laborer, after all.

There is a very gradual shading between the capitalist having many millions, and the laborer having nothing except his brains and limbs. One man has a vast fortune, another a hundred thousand dollars, another a quarter of that sum, another his farm, another his brains, one a store of goods, one a set of tools, another a shovel. Thus the gradations from the capitalist to the

* Technically, labor is exertion demanding something for itself in exchange.—PERRY. p. 122.

laborer shade off almost imperceptibly, and it is not easy to classify all persons.

As to the true relation between capitalist and laborer, there is scarce a division of opinion. Says Prof. PERRY :* "There is no sense or reason in the common jealousy of workmen towards employers. There is no real antagonism between them. Their interests lie along the same line. They are partners in the same concern." And this is the common language of all who have investigated the subject.

It may be very easily shown that the true interests of labor and capital are identical. Without the employment of capital, laborers in many cases could not live. An accumulation of capital is necessary to undertake most of the enterprises of the world. While a machine is being made, a railroad built, a crop raised, capital is required upon which to subsist. Without capital, people would live from hand to mouth, according to the common saying; that is, would return to their original state, and live by fishing, hunting, the fruits of the earth, and the like. It is by saving, accumulating capital, that the world has been able to make such progress—to build factories and railroads, and undertake thousands of enterprises, the returns upon which, though sure to come, may be long delayed.

The capitalist has the means to accomplish these things, if united with labor. He can do nothing without it. To build a railroad, labor is just as essential as capital. Both are indispensable elements. Hence the theoretical truth that they operate in perfect harmony. Were the rich man totally unable to unite his capital with labor, he would become a beggar; were the workman unable to get employment from the capitalist, he would

* *El. of Polit. Econ.*, p. 148, 5th ed.

starve. The interests of the two are, therefore, inseparably united; their need of each other is equally great.

What is their actual position? This is not a pleasant investigation to make. We shall present a dark picture of the motives ruling the greatest portion of mankind. Yet let it be remembered, that our investigation is general; it does not apply to every individual case. There are unselfish employers and laborers. We seek to analyze the motives which generally actuate the two classes. What are these?

The laborer is determined to get the highest wages for the least work; the employer the most work for the least wages.* The motives of the two classes are the same. The question of paying or receiving a reasonable compensation is not the one determining the question. How much can I get? how little can I pay? these are the questions asked.

The trades-unions of GREAT BRITAIN have declared this again and again. In the *Edinburgh Review*,† their object is clearly set forth: "'The final end' of the trades-unions is 'to raise to the highest practical point the rate of wages,' and it is their maxim that no work should be done heartily; to 'evade' work and to 'loiter' at work are rules; 'he who is most skillful in these arts is the greatest benefactor to his order;' 'the sluggard, according to the standard of the unions, must be the model workman;' the unionists have plans for making work that is useless to their employers; they, in some cases, oppose the use of machinery, and compel the public to make use of inferior articles—for example, hand-

---

* BURKE has said: " There is an implied contract, much stronger than any instrument or article of agreement, between the laborer in any occupation and his employer—that the labor, so far as that labor is concerned, shall be sufficient to pay to the employer a profit on his capital and a compensation for his risk; in a word, that the labor shall produce an advantage equal to the payment."—*Thoughts and Details on Scarcity*, vol. 5, p. 137.

† July No., 1868.

made bricks; the Leeds bricklayers have a rule against one man carrying more at a time than 'the ridiculously small number of eight bricks'; walking slowly to work, so as to consume as much as possible of the master's time, has been acted on as a rule; the trades-unions aim at 'making as much work as possible,' 'by rendering the labor of each less efficient;' the union is, in some cases, so 'omnipotent over masters,' that 'the industrial machine is turned topsy-turvy;' in cases of outrage, employers are afraid to prosecute, and a witness who appears in court against a trades-union, 'must be helped to emigrate.'"

This is, indeed, an extreme view. But it is the view of thousands. The workman is quite as selfish a being as his employer; we cannot credit him with having better motives.

What can the capitalist say for himself? Is he less selfish? Does he love his money less than those whom he employs? Let the long ecord, especially of British industry, answer. The capitalist has had the advantage of his workman, and he has rarely failed to use it. It is a hard truth that the world is forever trying to get advantage of each other. If all laborers were willing to work for a reasonable, or just price, and all capitalists were willing to pay it; if every exchanger were willing to buy and sell according to the same beautiful rule—the world would move on in perfect harmony. Unhappily, this is not the case. Every man seeks to get the most he can for what he sells, and pay as little as possible for what he buys. This is the law of the world. In order to carry out the law, all are forever inventing methods by which they can overreach each other, while the overreached are continually applying counter-protectives.

If a restrictive tariff law is enacted by which a railroad company pays twenty-five per cent. more for its rails, it makes up the advantage thus accruing to the home manufacturer by raising the price of freights.* If a man intends to buy anything, he hides his real intentions from the seller if he can. Why? Because he fears the seller will take advantage of the buyer's situation to raise the price. So men hide their real purposes, pretending not to want very badly, although their wants may be great; pretending to be not very desirous of selling, although wishing to sell even at a loss; and thus deceptions are employed; each afraid to tell the honest story of his condition, and trust his fellow, because he knows that, generally, men will take advantage of each other if they can. The capitalist is like the rest, and, unfortunately for the laboring class, he has an advantage over them which it is difficult for them to overcome. He can live if all his capital is not employed in reproduction; their labor will not keep, and, if they are not employed, they perish.

For example: A owns a factory run by a hundred hands. They demand higher wages and refuse to work until they be given. But the owner says: "No, I will stop my mill first." He has property besides, and can live upon that until it is exhausted; perhaps he has enough for his support always. But if the laborer does not work, he will starve. It is clear enough, then, that A holds his help in the hollow of his hand and can squeeze them as hard as he pleases. This is the fact, and every true observer will say so. Admitting the truth of all the beautiful theorizing about the necessary marriage of labor and capital in order to bring forth fruits for both, capital often has a decided advantage.

The laborer sees this. He says: "The capitalist has a great advantage over me, he can compel me to make a contract by

* See Col. GROSVENOR's admirable article on The Railroads and the Farms, as an illustration. *At. Monthly*, vol. 32, page 591.

which I am not fairly paid for my services." It is like telling a man to deliver up his money or forfeit his life. The capitalist says: "Work for me for so much or I will starve you to death."

And because he has this advantage over the laborer, most capitalists are not slow to avail themselves of it, and this is the cause of the enmity between the two classes.

The laboring class receive more sympathy because they are placed at the greatest disadvantage; they are not, in truth, a whit better than their employers, because, when they become wealthy, as many of them do, they quickly come to see things as other capitalists, and take up practices which once they condemned.

This is not an encouraging view of human nature, though it must be said, lest some one be deceived. Capitalist and laborer, each seeks to do the best he can for himself, each regards his interests as antagonistic to those of the other, each seeks to get every advantage over his opponent, but the capitalist is most favorably situated, he has more advantages, and can generally get the better half of the bargain with the laborer. This is the real situation of both classes.

In making the contract for labor, we maintain that the laborer ought to be willing to work for a reasonable price, and the employer ought to be willing to pay it; and each ought not to take advantage of the situation of the other. If labor be plenty, the employer ought to pay as much, other things with him remaining the same; if scarce, the employed ought to ask no advance of wages, provided his condition in other respects remains unchanged. In short, people ought not to take advantage of each other as they do.

This law men are violating continually. The capitalist declares that, as he is not bound to employ laborers at all, he has the right of paying them any price that may be agreed upon. In other words, as he is independent of the workman, he may pay him as little or as much as he pleases. The plea on behalf of the capitalist has been put by Mr. THORNTON,* in the following form: "Capital, being under no previous obligation to enter into arrangement with labor at all, is at liberty to reject any arrangement to which she objects, and is entitled to whatever profit may accrue to her from any arrangement to which labor and herself mutually agree. That the profit which thus accrues to capital may be fairly regarded as the produce of the labor by which the capital was created and which it represents, and would thus, in the absence of any agreement, belong entirely to capital, for the self-same reason for which unassisted labor is entitled to take as its reward the whole of its own produce." Is it true that the capitalist is under no obligation to enter into agreement with the laborer? Let us examine the question.

What are the relative positions of the two? Let the capitalist cease to employ the laborer, and how much capital has he left? Absolutely nothing. The laborer keeps him from sinking. Dispense with his services, and capital vanishes into thin air. Dispense with labor, and every vessel will rot at the wharves, every farm will run to weeds, the spindle will not give out its music. No man will have anything except what he can get by direct exertion. As for selling his property and living upon the income, who will buy if no labor can be employed? A great factory would not sell for a dollar, because it would be of no more use to the purchaser than the moon. That all desire to preserve their property and enhance its value, is a general truth which no one will deny. Of course, there are spendthrifts who have no ability or

* *On Labor,* page 13°.

desire to acquire property, or to keep what they may have inherited. But this is not true of mankind in general. Their desire is for more wealth, to save what they have and add to its value. These two facts then being true,—that all are intent upon saving their property, and that labor is absolutely necessary for this purpose,—the property-owner ought to be willing to pay a fair compensation for the labor whereby his riches are saved and increased.

Now, the usual way of looking at this question is this—no man is obliged to build a ship, or a factory, in order to employ labor, because he can loan his money to others. Very true, yet what do they want of it if they do not employ labor with it? If the manufacturer gets tired of his business and resolves to quit upon the ground that he is under no obligation to employ any one, he sells his establishment, and what then? Why, he invests his property in other concerns which employ labor. He employs and pays for labor less directly; that is the only difference. His money is put to the same use as before. He buys railroad stocks, but the railroad employs labor in great quantities. He puts it in a bank, but the bank employs labor, and loans its capital to others who use it for the employment of labor. Everywhere capital and labor touch, and if they do not, one is as worthless as the other. Whether employed directly, or loaned to others for them to use, capital must be employed in union with labor, else it is absolutely valueless. The man who is worth a million is as poor as the man not having a dollar, and both must get a living by simple and similar tasks. As men will not do that—as they will use their capital themselves, or loan it to others to be used by them—they are bound to pay a reasonable reward to the laborer for his services. The workman is just as necessary a factor in reproduction as capital, and rightfully stands upon an equal plane.

Again, the capitalist asks: "Have I not a right to do what I will with mine own? If I throw my capital away, surely I am under no obligation to employ workmen, for if I am, then all are bound to employ labor, whether having capital or not." If a man has nothing, he cannot be required to employ labor; if he has property, he is bound to use it, either directly or indirectly, for his own support and for the support of others. Can a portion of such property be used as capital in reproducing wealth, then it is a duty he owes to society to employ it so, or spend it in other ways. Government, in protecting property, thus enabling its owner to accumulate more, puts him under obligation to employ a portion of it in reproduction, as well as to spend another portion in the maintenance of himself. He has no right to throw it away. He must use it himself, or loan it to others to be used by them. For, if he will not use it himself or let others use it, his property becomes worthless, and the State is obliged to support him. The State has the right to see that no man wastes his property so as to become a burden to the public.

It is not necessary to go to this extreme length to defend our proposition. The truth is simply this—capital is utterly worthless unless joined with labor. Men are in fact bound to employ labor or else their possessions, whether great or small, are of no value to them or to any one else. Labor is just as necessary a factor in the saving and reproduction of capital, as in producing capital in the first place. Let it not be forgotten that in this whole discussion we are not talking of anything but labor, present and accumulated. Accumulated labor, to be worth anything, must be united with present labor; the two operate together. Consequently, the assertion is without foundation that the capitalist is under no obligation to employ labor. Such an obligation does exist. He has no right to throw his property away. We assume that every man is desirous of saving his property; if so, he must employ labor, else his property becomes valueless. And if he must employ labor to save it, he ought to pay a fair compensation therefor. Suppose a man's house was in danger of being carried away by a flood, and some men coming along were asked to help in saving it. They have no time to make a definite bargain as to the remuneration, but engage with a hearty will, and by their efforts save the house. Would not every one say that the owner of that house was mean if he were not willing to pay those men a reasonable compensation for their services? The position of the capitalist is the same in respect to his property. His capital will vanish like a stroke of lightning unless united with labor. Analyze the uses made of capital, and all cannot help admitting the fact. Labor is necessary to save property and enhance its value; if the owners of lands, factories, etc., are desirous of securing these ends, they must employ labor. Therefore they ought to pay a reasonable price for it.

As between workmen, there is a natural difference; one man is worth more than another, because he has greater strength or skill. It is right that the strongest and most skillful should receive higher wages. Concerning these natural advantages, there is nothing to be said. What we object to is the use of artificial and wrongful advantage. If the corn crop is less this year, the price should not be increased, except to require people to practice economy, or for some other good reason. If laborers are plentiful, let them be paid as much; if they are scarce, let them work for the old prices. Let no advantage be taken of unnatural, artificial, or forced conditions, and all will be well.

It will be said that this mode of reasoning is contrary to the operation of supply and demand. Shall that law cease to be applied? No, not in the true sense. All that we have written about asking and expecting reasonable prices, does not conflict with the working of this law. There is, however, a wide difference between the natural and unnatural operation of supply and demand. Rightly interpreted, the law is this—demand is what people really need and would purchase if they could buy at a reasonable price; and supply is the quantity that can be had at such a price. But the world is forever interfering with this law, by creating artificial scarcity on the one hand, and, on the other, by trying to make the demand less than it really is, so as to beat down the price. The law, to a great extent, does not express the truth about exchanges. The real demand is often much greater than purchases indicate, and the supply also. But people deceive each other; they exercise force, they refuse to sell when they really want to, hoping for an advance of prices. The buyer refuses to buy, although he really wants the thing, hoping to get a reduction of price. So numerous are the deceptions practiced, the real state of things is covered up so deeply, that the natural law of demand and supply has, in fact, only a limited operation.

What is a reasonable price depends upon many things. Obviously, it is impossible to draw any hard and fast line defining it. The most we can do is to find out what principle should govern in making contracts between capitalist and workman. This is a reasonable price without regard to any advantage which either capitalist or laborer might take of the condition of the other.

There are some considerations, however, that may be mentioned in making contracts for labor. First, the laborer should receive more where the work is hazardous to life and health, than in those occupations which are healthy and free from accident. An operative in a powder mill, or who makes certain parts of a brimstone match, ought to receive higher wages than a person working in a woolen factory, which is comparatively healthy and safe. Secondly, a person ought not to expect so much who receives regular employment as a person who cannot get work regularly. The ordinary hackman is justified in charging more for conveying passengers, if he can get them only now and then, than if he were employed all the time. The same person will charge less by the hour if he is to be employed for several hours, than if employed to go a short distance, in proportion to the time required. This is just. With a great many who work in factories, especially in New England, they ought not to expect so much, because their employers, in most instances, feel bound to give them constant employment if possible. Ofttimes they run, and at a loss, when they would not run, except to keep their help employed. Other considerations of less importance probably enter into the contract fixing the price of wages.

There are some subsidiary questions surrounding the main one which require notice. It is said, that labor is paid enough generally, whatever the price may be, because, as a class, workmen do not make a wise use of their wages.

That workmen are often prodigal in the use of their wages will not be denied. Since the war, the wages of factory operatives have remained nearly the same as before, the prices of living have been reduced, consequently operatives have reaped a fine harvest. Some of them have saved their money, though the larger number have spent it all. The goods in the factory stores and villages have changed in many respects, which is the best proof of the extravagance of this class. The amount of jewelry they wear is very large and expensive to what it was a few years ago. Their clothing, also, is costlier, and their living as well.

Now, it is said, why pay them so much? they do not make an economic use of their money; teach them to use it properly before giving it to them. This, by way of advice, is good. Operatives spend a great deal of money foolishly, and they should be taught to save it against a day of want, and for nobler uses. Yet is this a good defence to paying them higher wages?

The same mode of arguing will cut the manufacturer off from making money, for does he put it to any better use than his operatives? Is he not as extravagant, does he not spend as much money foolishly? He cannot, in truth, say anything on that score.

Thus we have gone over the ground between the capitalist and laborer, and sought to find out what is the true rule in the payment of labor. We do not say that the fixing of any price is always best; a division of the profits upon some agreed plan is preferable, whenever a division is practicable. It is not practicable in every case, and when it is not, this rule has a decided preference over every other. How various plans for rewarding labor have succeeded, and what efforts workmen have made to increase the price of wages, will be considered in the next chapter.

III.

ON THE INCREASE OF WAGES.

The history of the efforts to increase the price of labor is a very sad one. It is strewn with cruelty, injustice, and suffering. It is very instructive, however, and proves that amid the strifes and disappointments of contending parties, a better understanding has been created between them, and a nearer approximation to perfect justice, which will one day mark all their intercourse.

Workmen seek to secure their claims in the following ways: by first combining into societies, called trades-unions, and then demanding higher wages by conference with their employers, by councils of arbitration, and by strikes. The other ways of securing their rights are by forming industrial partnerships, and by abandoning the capitalist and forming co-operative associations. We shall consider, first, the methods of trades-union societies.

It is the largest voluntary organization in the world.* The

---

* The Amalgamated Society of Engineers in ENGLAND, a branch of the trades-unions, and numbering about 35,000 members, has an annual income of $440,000. The expenditures of the society from 1851 to 1868 were as follows:

Payments to members out of work	£425,844
Aids in sickness	161,388
For old age	45,272
For accidents	16,000
For burials	50,250
For extra fund for cases of special emergency	12,526
Aids to other trades	10,375
Total	£721,655

principal object of combining is to secure higher wages, while the incidental object is the support of workmen in sickness and destitution. The members are required to pay a certain sum per week to the organization, and this is expended in the support of strikers, sickness, etc.

The aim of trades-unions more specifically stated is, first, to oppose any reduction of wages; secondly, to cause a rise of wages whenever practicable; thirdly, to convert non-unionists into unionists, either by persuasion or coercion, the former means being preferred.* Besides these aims, they have sought to restrict their own competition in labor to certain limits deemed necessary to their welfare. The chief rules agreed upon to effect this object have been thus stated by Mr. Gostick:† "To insist on apprenticeship; to contend for the employment of workmen and apprentices in a certain ratio of their respective numbers; to oppose frequent, or 'systematic' working beyond the regular hours agreed on, and to prevent the employment of 'piece-masters.'" ‡

Leaving all other objects of the society out of sight except the principal one of raising the price of wages, workmen are entirely justified in uniting for this purpose so long as they pursue proper methods and do not make unreasonable demands. A considerable hostility has been displayed towards trades-unions, as they are considered the enemies of the capitalist. In one sense they are. The object of their creation is to increase the price of labor—in other words, to get a larger share of the capitalist's profits, which, in most instances, he is unwilling to give. In ENGLAND, especially, the greatest opposition to these societies has been exhibited. In

---

* *Ward's Workmen and Wages*, p. 18.
† *Cobden Club Essays*, p. 380, second series.
‡ "This 'piece-master' is a foreman, whose extra gains sometimes depend on extra pressure put upon the labor of those who work under his superintendence."—GOSTICK.

this country, labor is better rewarded and is more content. It is in ENGLAND that the laborer has fared worst, where the supply of labor is largest. Trades-unions have been more extensively organized there than in any other country; in ENGLAND has their power been most keenly felt.

It is just as evident that laborers have a right to combine in order to get their dues, as capitalists have to combine for the purpose of resisting an advance of wages. As long ago as when ADAM SMITH* wrote, he said that "masters are always and everywhere in a sort of tacit, but constant and uniform combination, not to raise the wages of labor above their actual rate. To violate this combination is everywhere a most unpopular action, and a sort of reproach to a master among his neighbors and equals."

Mr. THORNTON has reaffirmed the remark: "Large employers in any one extensive department of industry are not at all in the habit of competing with each other for labor. On the contrary, their custom is to deliberate together from time to time, in order to determine what wages it may, in existing circumstances, be advisable for them to offer, and some uniform rate is agreed to accordingly." †

It was a long period before workmen in ENGLAND were permitted to form these societies, so strongly entrenched were capitalists in the legislation of the realm. In 1799, the following act of Parliament shows the willingness of that body to legislate against the combination of workmen: "Contracts entered into for obtaining an advance of wages, for altering the usual time for working, or for decreasing the quantity of work (excepting such contract be made between a master and his journeyman), or preventing any person employing whomsoever they may think proper in their

* Vol. 1, p. 70, ROGERS' ed. † *West. Rev.*, vol. 81, p. 166, Am ed.

trade, or for controlling the conduct, or any way affecting any person or persons carrying on any manufacture or business, in the conduct or management thereof, shall be declared illegal, null and void."*

This statute illustrates how workmen were regarded in that day. Nor was it until 1827 that Parliament repealed all statutes prohibiting workmen from combining. Until then, employers and Parliament had taken it for granted that they alone could regulate the price of wages.

In having the right to combine acknowledged by Parliament, the cause of the workman was much advanced. He was for the first time put upon the same plane with the capitalist. They could now combine to work the price of labor up, as capitalists had hitherto combined to keep the price of labor down.

In this country, happily, we have never been troubled with this question. So far as our National or State Governments are concerned, workmen have no just cause of complaint. They have always been placed upon the same footing as the capitalist, and have enjoyed the unquestioned right to form trades-union societies. It is not until recently that the old doctrine of the right of the State to control the price of labor has been revived. This desire has been expressed by Governor BROWN, of Georgia. In his last annual message, he said that "labor must be controlled by law. We may hold inviolate every law of the UNITED STATES, and still so legislate upon our labor system, or in lieu of that, establish a baronial one." We imagine that there is no danger of the old English law being re-enacted on this republican soil. Liberty to contract for labor is too deeply grounded to be crushed out by the fiat of Gov. BROWN, or by any one else of his way of thinking.

* 40 GEORGE III, chap 90.

In this country trades-unions are of less account, because workmen, as a general thing, are well paid. So long as there is so much unimproved land to be easily had, the claims of labor will get a fair hearing. The western prairies are an asylum to which the laborer may, at any time, fly from the face of his oppressors.

Three ways there are, as we have said, by which trades-unions seek to get an advance of wages: by conference with their employers, by councils of conciliation, and by strikes. Concerning the latter mode we will speak first.

Strikes, which in the fourteenth century had their counterpart in the Jacquerie riots, are the last thing for the laborer to resort to in order to get an advance of wages. As for the justice of them, if workmen are not getting a reasonable price for their work, and their employers refuse to pay more, after working the length of time agreed upon, they are justified in quitting their places. That is all there is in the phenomena of strikes, refusal to work unless an advance be paid, and the workman has a perfect right to demand such a price and to quit working unless the advance be offered.*

In ENGLAND, and we believe the same is true in this country, workmen, generally, have oftener struck to resist a fall than to secure a rise of wages. Says Mr. BRASSEY,† "Resistance to a proposed reduction was the cause of the engineers' strike in 1852; of the strike at Preston in 1853; of the strike in the iron trade in 1865; and of the strike of the colliers, at Wigan, in 1868. In

---

* Mr. THORNTON has considered the ethics of strikes fully in a paper published in the *West. Rev.* upon Strikes and Industrial Co-operation; vol. 81, pp. 165—67. Some able and interesting observations upon this subject are contained in a paper by FREDERIC HARRISON entitled The Iron-Masters' Trades-Union, *Fort. Rev.*, vol. 1, p. 96.

† *Work and Wages*, p. 6.

each of these cases, the masters had found it necessary, in consequence of the depressed state of trade, to reduce the rate of wages: but the men, ignoring the circumstances of the trade, and looking only to what they believed to be a degradation of their position as workmen, refused to accept the reduction."

Although in many cases workmen have failed to get higher wages, yet not always. One of the principal reasons given for GREAT BRITAIN's failure to supply iron manufactures to this and other countries, is the very large advance in the price of labor occasioned by the strikes of trades-union societies. The London Times,* in a recent editorial on the decline of the English iron trade with the UNITED STATES, remarked that the price of iron depended very materially upon the price of coal. Anything that raises the price of coal affects the price of iron. "Now," says that journal, "without pronouncing judgment on the disputed question whether strikes have been the exclusive cause of the late rise of coal in ENGLAND, we may take it as granted that they have been a very principal cause, and that they are now exercising a controlling influence in keeping up the admittedly excessive price."

Strikes, in this country, have not been very serious or long protracted. They have occurred in almost every branch of trade; in the cotton and woolen mills, among the coal mines, engineers of railways have occasionally struck, masons, carpenters, printers, and others. The coal-mine strikes have been the most extensive and expensive of any. Mr. THORNTON has summed up the result of some of the numerous strikes in ENGLAND, happening within the last twenty-five years, but a detailed account of them, and many others besides, will be found in *Ward's Workmen and Wages*. We

' Aug. 29, 1873.

shall merely mention the great strike of the Manchester spinners in 1829, when $1,250,000 wages were forfeited; the Ashton and Staleybridge strikes of 1829 and 1830, participated in by 30,000 spinners and who lost $1,250,000; the strikes of the Tyne and Wear pitmen in 1832, which were very protracted; the Manchester builders' strike in 1833, when $360,000 of wages were lost; the "terrible" strikes of the Preston spinners; first, in 1836, lasting thirteen weeks and costing the men $286,000; and secondly, in 1854, when 17,000 persons went into voluntary idleness, suffering intensely for thirty-six weeks, and giving up $2,100,000 wages; the engineers' strike in 1853, of fifteen weeks' duration, in which $215,000 wages were sacrificed; the strike in the metropolitan building trade in 1860; and the strikes of the iron workers of Staffordshire and the North in 1865, and of the London tailors in 1868; these are a few of the more prominent instances.

Before resorting to strikes, workmen, in many cases, seek to settle their differences with their employers by arbitration. Ofttimes a hearing is had, both parties state their claims, and the arbitrator renders a decision, which is accepted as final by both parties. These courts of conciliation have been the authors of an immense amount of good, and prevented numerous strikes. The employer, by coming forward at these times and making a full showing of his business—what he can afford to pay and what not —has saved both himself and his workmen from many a rupture and loss of work and profits.

This mode of settling disputes between employer and employed originated in FRANCE, and is there termed Conseils des Prud'hommes. They are established by decree of government, and consist of a president, vice-president, who can be neither workmen nor employers, and six members elected by both classes. The proceedings are inexpensive, the judges not being paid; and a delegation of the council, consisting of one employer and one workman, sit in judgment almost daily. "The result," says BRASSEY,* "in ninety-five out of one hundred cases brought before these tribunals, is a reconciliation between the parties; and, though appeals are permitted to the superior courts of law, they are rarely made. . . In 1850, 28,000 disputes had been heard before the Conseils des Prud'hommes, of which no less than 26,800 were satisfactorily settled."

Little has been said about the establishment of courts of conciliation in this country, yet they have produced so much peace abroad, that, were the tribunal established here, it probably would yield the best results. When a division between the two classes has actually broken out, these courts can do little, perhaps, to make peace; but if they are instituted early enough, they are likely to save many a bitter and expensive contest between the capitalist and his workmen.

Having shown how the workman seeks to increase his wages by strikes, we turn to another side of the same subject to present the experience of improving his lot by co-operation. This is of two kinds: first, co-operation of workmen simply; secondly, co-operation with capitalists, which latter method of conducting business is termed an industrial partnership. We shall not tarry long with either of these topics and do little more than point out a few results, for the history of these movements has been related so many times, that the public are quite well informed of it already.

The birth of the first co-operative society occurred in Rochdale nearly thirty years ago. The organization was called the Rochdale Pioneers. The history of the society has been told in a most

* *Work and Wages*, p. 272.

attractive way by Mr. THORNTON in his work *On Labor*. The rise of this society was like the growth of a mustard seed. In the beginning, twenty-eight flannel weavers, disgusted with the poor quality and outrageous price of the provisions they were in the habit of buying, subscribed two and three pence a week towards making up a sum of twenty-eight pounds, which they spent in purchasing, at wholesale prices, in Manchester, flour, sugar, butter, and oatmeal. From this common stock, each took what he wanted at the current prices, paying in cash; and when the whole amount had been sold, they were surprised to find that so much had been made by the operation. They repeated the experiment. They purchased in larger quantities and added to their subscribers. The embryo association was laughed at in the beginning, but it continued to grow, and after a short time it was found that a room was necessary to hold the goods purchased. A small one was hired, and it was arranged that one of their number should act as salesman for a few hours during two evenings in the week. In 1845, the second year of the society, the number of subscribers had increased from twenty-eight to seventy-four, and the capital was £181, upon which a net benefit of £32 had accrued. The two following years they divided £80 and £77; and they have gone on increasing at a wonderful rate ever since. In 1847, linen and woolen drapery was added to the original grocery and chandlery business; in 1850, a butcher's shop was grafted on; shortly after, a slaughter-house; in 1852, shoemaking and tailoring were begun. A single glance at the profits tells the story of progress. We have not space for all the figures; we will simply show what they were at the end of each period of five years. The society was started in 1844, and the net profits run as follows:

1845,	£22	....	1848,	£117	....	1860,	£15,906
1846,	80	....	1849,	561	....	1865,	25,156
1847,	72	....	1850,	880	....	1867,	41,619
			1855,	3,106			

The causes of their success are very clearly seen. They bought at wholesale, and always paid in cash, thus getting the largest discounts. They never sold on credit, and consequently had no bad debts. Having a large number of shareholders, they were assured of plenty of customers, and were under no necessity of spending a penny to make themselves known in order to obtain trade. The expenses of management were small, not exceeding two per cent. of the business done. For attracting outsiders, their equitable distribution of profits was a device far more efficacious than a showy front or advertising.

When any one makes a purchase, he receives a tin ticket, whether a member of the association or not, denoting the sum he has paid. At the end of every quarter, when profits are declared, there is a deduction of five per cent. per annum, for interest on the capital, another deduction of two and one-half per cent. as an education fund is taken out, and the balance is divided among the holders of the tickets.

There are some very decided benefits arising from this form of co-operation. First, one's money goes farther than anywhere else; secondly, the stores give the best possible security to the purchaser that what he buys will be of the best quality, since it is the same as the owners of the concern purchase for themselves. Upon these points Mr. HOLYOAKE * has justly said: "The whole

* *Self-Help*, pp. 38-9. He also says: "They have no interest in chicanery. Their sole duty is to give fair measure, full weight, and pure quality, to men who never knew before what it was to have a wholesome meal, whose shoes let in water a month too soon, whose waistcoats shone with devil's dust, and whose wives wore calico that would not wash. These men now buy in the market like millionaires, and, as far as pureness of food goes, live like lords. They make their own shoes, sew their own garments, and grind their own corn. They buy the purest sugar

atmosphere of a store is honest. In that market there is no distrust and no deception—no adulteration and no second prices. Buyer and seller meet as friends. There is no overreaching on the one side, and no suspicion on the other."

Besides supplanting dearer and poorer shops, co-operative stores stimulate to self-amendment and promote prudence. The poorer class, considering the means they have, are not infrequently quite as wasteful and extravagant as others; but these societies have a most beneficial effect in the way of elevating all concerned, and making them prudent and more self-reliant men.*

The other form of co-operation is that of industrial partnership. This is the more natural method, because capital is brought in to the aid of labor.†

The idea of an industrial partnership is for the capitalist to give the workmen wages, a sum rather low, enough to sustain themselves by living prudently, and then, after deducting a certain sum for the use of the capital, to divide the rest of the profits, if any there be, upon certain terms agreed upon between the employer and his employees. The most successful industrial establishments in GREAT BRITAIN are the Methley collieries, owned by HENRY BRIGGS, SON & CO., and several slate quarry organizations in WALES.‡ The first of these organizations is worthy of a brief description. The business of the proprietors was undertaken in 1852. For the next twelve years their relations with their men

<small>and the best tea, and grind their own coffee. They slaughter their own cattle, and the finest beasts of the land waddle down the streets of Rochdale, for the consumption of flannel-weavers and cobblers."

* An article by Prof. FAWCETT upon the Position and Prospects of Co-operation, in the February No. of *Fort. Rev.*, 1874. is worth reading in this connection. Also one by THOMAS HUGHES upon The Working Classes of Europe. *Inter. Rev.*, March, 1874.

† In GERMANY, workmen form associations and the State and banks loan them money to be used in the prosecution of their business. This is also done by the French Government to a limited extent.

‡ For a description of the slate quarries see *Cairnes' Essays on Polit. Econ.*, p. 166.</small>

were most unsatisfactory, and strikes were constantly occurring. In 1865, they launched their experiment of an industrial partnership. The business of the firm was transferred to a joint-stock company, the owners retaining two-thirds of the shares, and offering the other third to the public, and especially inviting their employees to become shareholders. At the same time they arranged "that whenever the divisible profits accruing from the business, after a fair and usual reservation for redemption of capital and other legitimate allowances, exceeded ten per cent. on the capital embarked, all those employed by the company as managers, agents, or work-people, should receive one-half of such excess profit as a bonus, to be distributed among them as a per centage on their respective earnings during the year in which such profit should have accrued."

They made no claim to disinterestedness; they adopted the system as one of convenience and speculation. Their profits had never exceeded ten per cent., and these they were sure of receiving before there was any division to the employees.

The undertaking proves that the BRIGGS reasoned well. The experiment has been a brilliant success. All the expectations based upon it have been realized, and some unlooked-for advantages have accrued. The trial began July 1, 1865. "At the end of the first twelve-month the total of profits was found to be fourteen per cent., of which the shareholders took twelve and the work-people two per cent. In the second year the total was sixteen per cent., the shareholders getting thirteen per cent. and the workpeople three. In the third year the corresponding figures were seventeen and three and a-half."*

Industrial partnerships are the consummate flower of the war

---

* THORNTON *On Labor*, p. 352.

between labor and capital. Men like profits better than salaries. We suspect this is the outcropping of the speculative or gambling spirit which every person displays in some degree. It is only fair, though, since workmen add their full share to the increase of capital, that the division of such increase be equitable. It is the best stimulus to workmen—they put forth their best energies—and it is the fairest mode of conducting business whenever possible. The whale fisheries have always been conducted on this principle. It is worthy of more attention than it has received, for it reveals the true relationship that should exist between the capitalist and the workman. They join hands, brains, and strength, for the same common end, to produce more wealth, and to make a fair division thereof between them.

The unity of the relation between the two classes is being more clearly seen, and the enmity between them is slowly, but surely, disappearing. Can we not see in vision as THORNTON has seen—

> " * * * of shadows thrown before
> Coming events, things that surely be,
> Nor now delayed, but until man, no more
> Wholly on blinding lust intent, shall see
> That his whole interest and his kind's are one,
> Blended in individual destiny."

IV.

EFFECT OF MACHINERY ON LABOR.

Wealth is increased in one of three ways—by transmutation, by transportation, and by transformation. The first way is that of the agriculturalist; the second of the merchant and carrier; the third, the manufacturer and mechanic's.

In each of these three ways, the most important principle, especially in the latter way, of increasing wealth, is by the proper division of employments. This portion of the field of political economy has been fully explored by able writers, though perhaps no one since ADAM SMITH has made so many discoveries in it as CHARLES BABBAGE, in his *Economy of Manufactures*. Among the three advantages of dividing employments mentioned by SMITH, is the invention of machinery. Some of the effects, direct and remote, flowing from its use may be noticed, as they have not been fully described.

One effect is the continued hostility on the part of workmen to the introduction of all machinery superseding labor. This hostility is nothing compared to what it was in former times. "Yet there are a considerable number of the working-classes who have a lingering, lurking dislike to machinery, which they cannot rationally explain, and who look with the liveliest apprehension at any improvement which may be effected in that grand aid to human industry." * Mr. WARD† intensifies this truth by referring to the riot at Coventry, ENGLAND, which arose from the attempt to apply steam-power in the manufacture of ribbon; and to the opposition at Northampton, Kettering, and Wellingboro', over the introduction of sewing-machines in the manufacture of boots and shoes. Another good authority has affirmed that hundreds of inventions are not utilized because trades-unions are opposed to their use, and are powerful enough to have their way. Millions of bad bricks are made annually, because this society will not permit the use of brick-making machinery. No spirit of injurious opposition to the use of labor-saving machinery has appeared in this country, nor has any occasion happened to rouse opposition, as there has always been a flood-tide of work for every one. May this spirit always prevail here, for the sake of the workman and all.

It cannot be denied that labor-saving machinery displaces labor. It must do so during some period of its use else the name is a false one. As a railway engine will do the work of many horses, thus superseding the use of the noble animal, so the horse has superseded the work of thousands of men, because, in many ways, it can accomplish more.

The invention of machinery has been more wonderful in this country than in any other. This is owing, principally, to the scarcity of labor, though partly to the greater skill of the mechanics. It is worthy of note how the strikes in ENGLAND are leading the manufacturers to develop more perfectly the use of machinery there. This was mentioned by Mr. NASMYTH, a noted English manufacturer, in his evidence given before the Trades-union Commissioners. His desire to invent labor-saving machinery was

---

* EDMUND POTTER; paper read at Social Science Meeting, Glasgow, 1868.
† *Workmen and Wages*, p. 240.

increased by a strike, in 1851, affecting his business. By new contrivances invented since that time, he had been able to reduce the number of men from fifteen hundred to one-half as many.

"That machinery does not diminish, but enlarges the field of employment," says one author, "is a thesis which he would be ashamed to argue." We are sure the statement cannot be received without explanation. Did no new cause operate upon the introduction of machinery except a reduction in the price of the product, the field of employment would certainly be diminished.* Let a machine be invented by which half the labor required to make a particular thing is displaced. Let the future price of it be reduced in proportion to the diminished cost of manufacture. Will the demand double so that the men first thrown out of employment will be subsequently employed in the same business?

* The economy often wrought through the use of machinery is remarkable. During the recent war, the English developed their machinery for making fabrics more than ever before during the same time, and reduced, to a considerable extent, the amount of labor required to run it, as the following table shows:

COTTON FACTORIES.

	1856.	1861.	1868.
No. of Factories	2,210	2,387	2,549
No. of Spindles	28,010,217	30,387,467	32,000,014
No. of Power Looms	298,847	399,992	379,329
No. of Persons Employed	379,213	451,569	401,064

WOOLEN, WORSTED AND SHODDY FACTORIES.

	1856.	1861.	1868.
No. of Factories	2,030	2,211	2,465
No. of Spindles	3,111,521	3,471,781	6,455,879
No. of Power Looms	53,399	64,818	118,865
No. of Persons Employed	166,885	173,046	253,056

FLAX, HEMP AND JUTE FACTORIES.

	1856.	1861.	1868.
No. of Factories	417	440	472
No. of Spindles	1,288,043	1,252,236	1,679,357
No. of Power Looms	8,689	15,347	35,047
No. of Persons Employed	80,262	94,003	135,333

By no means. In fact, if such a saving in the cost of production takes place, a long period ensues, generally, before the purchaser gets the full benefit of the improved machinery.

It does not follow, though, that the workman fares worse, in the end, from the introduction of machinery. The fruit of his brain is not bitterness to his body. By inventing machinery and economizing labor, he does not dig his own grave. Far from it. Labor is released, by the use of machinery, for a season; afterwards, it all returns.

In what way? By cheapening the price of products, and, from the increase of national wealth, the demand is enlarged.* Hence, a larger supply must be had. It is this second cause joined to the first which crowds the demand, in many things, upon the heels of the producer as sharply as ever. When the sewing-machine was invented, it was believed that thousands of women would thereafter find no work. What has happened? First, a larger amount of clothing is demanded, because the cost of making it is less; secondly, the amount of sewing upon some things has largely increased; thirdly, there is more wealth with which to pay for clothing and sewing. Has the invention of the steam engine driven men out of employment? Whether in transportation, or other business, it has been the means of multiplying the demand for labor. Not only do workmen continue to be employed since the introduction of machinery, but also at better rates; while others find work, because some of the processes of production are greatly simplified. Workmen can be employed to make parts of locomotives which once were made only by artisans. Thousands are employed in factories for making cloth, who never would have been employed if all the processes of making were undertaken by

* THORNTON, *on Labor*, p. 319.

one person. Machinery has introduced an infinite number of simple processes.

In respect to the increased pay derived from working machinery, it is difficult to give figures without a great deal of explanation, because the price of wages has been increased from other causes besides this.*

From these, and many other facts, it is clear that machinery is not the enemy of workmen. Let the opposition to its introduction cease. May the workman continue to apply his skill in producing new machinery and in running the old, with the confident hope that he is sure of earning his bread and robbing no one of it, not less when he works with the mute wisdom of machinery, than when wearing out his own fingers. "No trades-unions," says EDMUND POTTER, "ever encouraged invention." This is a sad fact. Machinery has brought a thousand comforts to millions who would otherwise have been denied them, and what workman to-day can trace his lack of employment, if out of it, to the introduction of machinery?

It may be asked, will not the augmented power of machinery ultimately reduce the quantity of labor. We think not. It certainly will in particular employments, but the labor thus released will take up new occupations. The demand for most things has

* In *Porter's Progress of the Nation*, p. 197, he gives an interesting table of the prices of the wages of spinners, and their cost of living for a long period, which we quote:

Work of Spinner.		Wages	Hours of	Flour	Flesh	Week's Net earnings would purchase	
Years.	per week.	per week.	work	per sack.	per lb.	Lbs.	Lbs.
	Lbs. Nos.	s. d.	per week.	s. d.		Flour.	Flesh.
1804,	12 . 180	32 6	74	83 0	..6d. to 7d...	117 .	62½
1804,	9 . 200	36 6	74	83 0	.. 6 to 7..	124	73
1814,	18 . 180	44 6	74	70 6	8 ..	175	67
1814,	13½ . 200	60 0	74	72 6	8 ..	239	90
1833,	22½ . 180	33 8	69	45 0	6	210 .	67
1833,	19 . 200	42 9	69	45 0	6	267 .	85

a practical limit, and when production reaches that, it must stop. That over-production is not possible in all branches of industry at once, though possible in some, is a doctrine which few, if any, will deny. But human wants cannot cease entirely so long as man lives.

Another effect springing from the invention and use of machinery is the rise of large factories.* Machinery first diminishes labor and increases gains, unless the price of the thing sold is reduced correspondingly with the diminished cost of production. Sometimes, a manufacturer prefers to sell at the old price and increase his profits in that way; sometimes, by reducing the price and stimulating the demand. His preference will be for that way which is likely to yield him the greatest profits. If the demand increases, as in many things it does, whether prices are reduced or not, the manufacturer enlarges his factory to produce more and enhance his profits. This, of course, does not logically follow, but if a business is profitable in the beginning and machinery is invented whereby the profits are increased, generally the manufacturer increases his capacity for production to that point where he can manufacture at the greatest profit; extending his business so far as to be dependent upon the smallest number not employed by himself in producing his wares. For example, some of the railroads are constructing rolling mills to produce their own rails, because it is cheaper than to buy of others. This practice of extending the manufacture of things so as to cover as many processes as possible, is growing every day. A lock manufacturer, for example, instead of purchasing his castings of another, will make them himself. And thus the process goes on of combining more and more, under the ownership of one person, the different processes involved in a given product.

* See *West. Rev.*, vol. 81, p. 164, Am. ed.

It is not within our purpose to state how far this combination of processes has been carried, but simply the effect of it, both upon workmen and the public.

One effect is a tendency to diminish the price of manufactured products. Why does the lock manufacturer make his castings instead of purchasing them of the foundryman? Either, because he can make better ones at the same price, or similar castings at a lower price. In short, because he can save money by the operation. If he can, he can afford to sell his wares at a reduced price. Whether he will or not depends upon the state of facts previously indicated—whether he can make more by selling the same quantity at larger profits, or a larger quantity at profits reduced. A combination of processes generally tends to a reduction of the price of things.

Again, if the price is not diminished in the first instance, the great gains realized tempt others to rush into the business, unless it be a legal monopoly, and, through force of competition, prices are diminished.

V.

ON THE MEANING AND CAUSES OF VALUE.

The saying is reported of PRODICUS, the master of SOCRATES, that "a right use of words is the beginning of knowledge." Yet words rightly used are very imperfect signs to express ideas. The same words, phrases, and sentences convey dissimilar notions to different persons and there is no way of overcoming the difficulty.

Words are absolutely necessary for the conveyance of ideas, and a definition is nothing more than a combination of them. However imperfect, therefore, definitions may be, no progress in the acquisition of knowledge can be made without them.

Acting upon the principle enunciated by PRODICUS, the Greek school of sophists, led principally by himself, PROTAGORAS, and HIPPIAS, devoted themselves to the study of words with great assiduity, and the flowering of this impulse is found in the works of ARISTOTLE, whose terminology is exceedingly clear.* Great attention was paid to this subject till the time of DESCARTES, who went to the other extreme and declared that words had no fixed meaning at all.†

* See *Grant's Aristotle*, vol. 1, pp. 81–9.
† *Hallam, Lit. of Europe*, vol. 1, 102.

A complete dictionary would comprise the sum total of human knowledge. Such a work is like a great field, each word answering to a lot, and the entire number of lots comprising the whole field. Now, as additional fences may be built, or old ones pulled down, so that the lots may become smaller or larger, words may be defined as having a narrower or wider meaning. Indeed, one might continue to widen the meaning of a word till the whole circle of human knowledge was embraced within it.

Let the reader think this subject over carefully and he cannot fail to reach the conclusion that a definition is an elastic thing, stretched by one and contracted by another—an arbitrary proceeding which cannot be changed. The most that can be said for the definition of a thing is, that more persons will define or describe it in one particular way; it is the number and quality of noses assenting to a given definition which render it more authoritative than another; but there is no test by which a definition can be declared true, whatever be the authority assenting to it. Yet the farmer must fence his land to indicate where it is, so words must be defined, bounded, to give them any significance.

As value is the root-term of economic science, it is necessary to define the meaning in which it is to be used. Whether corresponding to the meaning given by others or not, such a course is necessary in order to make any progress with the several topics we propose to consider. Were this not done, we should be as completely lost as a ship at sea upon a starless night, without compass or guide to point the way.

Although the term "value" plays a most conspicuous part in political economy, yet many economic writers have neglected to define it carefully, as though the term were of little importance. In consequence of this neglect, they have greatly multiplied the errors to be found in this department of study, which were numerous enough before.

At the outset, we remark that value is not a quality inhering in any object whatever. This truth will appear very clearly from Professor Perry's illustration. "If I take up a new lead-pencil from my table, for the purpose of examining all its qualities, I shall immediately perceive those which are visible and tangible. The pencil has length, a cylindrical form, a black color, is hard to the touch, is composed of wood and plumbago in certain relations to each other, and has the quality, when sharpened at the end, of making black marks upon white paper. These qualities, and such as these, may be learned by a study of the pencil itself. But can I learn, by a study of the pencil itself, the *value* of the pencil? Is value a quality? By any examination of its mechanical, or by any analysis of its chemical, properties, can I detect how much the pencil is *worth?* No. The questioning of the senses, however minute, the test of the laboratory, however delicate, applied to the pencil alone can never determine how much it is worth."* Value, then, is not a quality of a thing. It can never be found in any object. The mistakes of economists who have not kept this truth clearly in view have been most deplorable.

Before going further towards finding out the meaning of value, let us stop to define utility. This is the capacity of an object to satisfy the desire of its possessor. But the utility here meant is not "that utility which is determined by reason and measured by a philosophical standard."† If an object has capacity to satisfy the desire of its possessor, however strong or weak, however depraved or elevated the desire may be, that object has utility. In this sense of the word, which is the etymological one, ardent

---
* *Elements of Polit. Econ.*, p. 46. † Bowen, *Am. Polit. Econ.*, p. 72.

spirits have utility the same as wheat. An obscene book, so long as it satisfies desire, has utility,—like the Bible which satisfies the longing of many a soul. The same thing may have no utility to one man, a low utility to another, and a very high utility to a third. That is, it has no capacity to satisfy the desire of the first, a slight capacity to satisfy the desire of the second, but a very high capacity to satisfy the desire of the other.*

Utility must be carefully distinguished from exchangeability. Utility is the capacity of an object to satisfy the desire of its owner; exchangeability is the capacity of an object to satisfy the desire of one not the owner, combined, also, with his ability to purchase it. Hence, an object may have utility even though no one besides the owner ever hears of its existence; an object never has exchangeability unless known to and desired by another.

An article may possess both exchangeability and utility. This is often the case. Thus gold is exchangeable, for it may be desired by another; and also useful, for the owner may wear it as ornament or otherwise, or manufacture it into watches, jewelry, and the like. Having cleared up the meaning of these terms, let us proceed on our way towards defining value.

When ROBINSON CRUSOE recovered from his shipwreck, he found that he was the sole owner and occupant of a comfortable and fertile island. There was abundance for food and clothing; he easily provided himself with a house for shelter and habitation. Yet all these possessions had no value. They had utility, for they could satisfy his wants. Indeed, they were quite as useful to him as if he and they had been in ENGLAND. Their utility was great, their value nothing; why did they not have value? The presence of some other person was necessary having exchangeable

* See *Perry's El. of Polit. Econ.*, p. 7 .

objects, and wanting also some of Crusoe's things; and further, an exchange must have actually taken place before the commodities of either person could have had any value. If people living in the same community, and owning different commodities, never exchanged them with each other, such commodities would have no value. Commodities cannot have value unless their owners exchange them with one another for those things which they desire, but have not. Consequently, Crusoe's possessions had no value, because he owned everything and was alone. If another person had lived there, having various things Crusoe wanted, and which could have been obtained by exchanging a part of his own for them, then the values of the several commodities exchanged could have been ascertained. Hence we find that the value of a commodity is an estimate agreed to between the person parting with and the person receiving it.

In what words or terms is this estimate or value expressed? A has a hat and B a pair of shoes. Each wishes to exchange his product for that of the other. After considerable discussion, in which A declares that he ought to have more than the shoes for his hat, it is agreed that each shall exchange his product for that of the other. The value of the hat, therefore, is expressed by the shoes; thus the hat is said to be worth the pair of shoes; and, likewise, the shoes are worth the hat. The value of each product is expressed by the other. Thus, our conception of value is now complete, and may be expressed in the following manner: Value is the estimate agreed to between the person parting with, and the person receiving a commodity, expressed in some other commodity that is exchanged for it.*

---

* When one commodity is exchanged for another, each measures the value of the other.— *J. R. McCulloch, Encyc. Brit., Art. Money.*

This definition of value will be easily apprehended. It will be seen that value does not reside in a commodity; it is an estimate or affection of the mind. It is not an estimate made by one person, however, but by two or more—by all the parties owning the several articles that are exchanged. Nor is an estimate ever the value of anything unless an exchange actually takes place.

Hence, an *ex parte* estimate, i. e., the estimate of one person, or the estimates of persons who are not the owners, can never be considered as the value of anything. True, we can tell what the value of a commodity was at the time of the last exchange, as expressed in the commodity exchanged for it. We can tell what it probably will exchange for at some future time. And this is our meaning when we say that a commodity is worth a certain sum or thing. We mean that it was exchanged for some other thing, or can be exchanged for it at some future time. So the merchant, conscious of this truth, can calculate with a reasonable degree of certainty upon the wants of his customers, and what he can probably get for his goods. And because the values or estimates men put upon things undergo but little change they can buy and sell, and engage in commerce in the most distant parts of the earth. Yet how often men fail to discern the varying and capricious values or estimates that will be put upon things, is a matter of common experience.

MACLEOD has done much to clear up the meaning of value, yet he has made some mistakes. Thus, he says that, " however much a person may wish to sell any product of his own, yet, if no one will buy it, it has no value. If an exchange takes place, it can only do so from the reciprocal desire of each for the product of the other. Hence, it is clear that *value necessarily requires the concurrence of two minds.*"* It is a little singular, however, that he

* *Theory and Practice of Banking*, vol. 1, p. 14.

should have written the following sentence just before those quoted: "We may observe that since a thing which cannot be exchanged has no value, the value of anything depends not upon the person who offers it for sale, but upon the desire of the purchaser."
Is not this equivalent to saying that the value of a thing depends upon the desire of the purchaser? And is not this statement directly opposed to the one previously quoted, namely, "that value necessarily requires the concurrence of two minds, ... and that if an exchange takes place, it can only do so from the reciprocal desire of each for the product of the other"? Before an exchange can take place, there must be a meeting of minds; which person has the strongest desire to exchange is often difficult to tell, for each generally tries to conceal his desires in part, at least, in the hope of making a better exchange. Suppose the purchaser is in great want of bread, and the seller knows it, will not the latter use his information to increase the value or estimate of his bread? Or suppose a dealer has some article on hand like perishable fruit, which he is very desirous to dispose of, will not the purchaser often use his knowledge to reduce the value of the fruit? Consequently, the statement is a mistake that "the value of anything depends, not upon the person who offers it for sale, but upon the desire of the purchaser." It depends upon the desires of both; which of them has the strongest or weakest desire cannot easily be told.

An invariable standard of value is impossible. For, supposing that the values of two commodities have changed relatively to each other since a former exchange, in which commodity has the change taken place? Thus, suppose a bushel of wheat was exchanged for a dollar of gold last year, and that two bushels must be given for a dollar this. Has the gold risen in value or that of the wheat declined? It is no nearer the truth to say that the wheat has declined than that the gold has risen. Suppose that ten commodities have each been exchanged for the same amount of gold for a hundred years. This year, however, one of them, sugar, for example, is exchanged for twice as much gold as ever before. Has sugar, therefore, risen in value, or has the value of gold declined? Put any examples you like, it will always be found that value is a relative expression, and, consequently, that no object can ever have a greater or less value than that with which it is compared and exchanged. Professor FAWCETT has stated this truth correctly; "When the general value of a commodity declines, less of every commodity can be obtained for it in exchange; but if this be so, the value of all these commodities must rise, when compared with the particular commodity in the value of which it has been supposed a general decline has taken place. These considerations demonstrate the erroneous nature of a statement not unfrequently made, that there is a general rise or fall in the value of all commodities. . . . . It is quite impossible that there should be a general rise of values, for if there is a rise in the value of one commodity, there must be a fall in the value of all the commodities with which this one is compared."* The works of ADAM SMITH and RICARDO are badly infected with error in consequence of their failure to see this truth. Both sought after an invariable standard of value, which every living political economist admits cannot be found.

Before quitting this branch of our subject we may define the meaning of price. It is the value of a commodity expressed in money. Thus BASCOM says that "the price of anything is its power to command gold, silver, or that which constitutes the cur-

* *Manual of Polit. Econ.* p. 270.

rency of the country. Value may be expressed in any commodity whatever: price is expressed in one commodity only."*

We are now ready to consider the causes of value. What are the causes leading men to agree to the values of articles bought and sold?

It has been the custom among political economists to treat of the causes of value instead of those of price, yet as exchanges in all civilized countries are generally expressed in money, our investigation will be simplified if we consider the causes of price rather than those of value. In so doing, this assumption is involved, which must be kept in view, that when the price of a commodity varies, the variation is always supposed to be produced by something which affects the value of the commodity, and not the value of money. Let us explain our meaning by an illustration. Suppose it is observed that the price of wheat rises; this rise in the price of wheat may be due to two very distinct causes. In the one case wheat may become scarcer, and therefore dearer; in the other case, wheat, in common with every other commodity, may rise in price, in consequence of new discoveries of the precious metals, such as those made in AUSTRALIA and CALIFORNIA during the last few years. In the following investigation, the assumption is made that variations in price are not caused by an alteration in the value of money.

What, then, are the causes of price? They are four, namely, difficulty of attainment, exchangeability, personal effort, and willingness of deprivation.

By difficulty of attainment is meant the labor or other difficulty inhering in, or connected with, a commodity which a person who is not the owner desires, and which he had rather buy than per-

* *Polit. Econ.*, p. 222.

form the labor of attaining directly himself. Hence, if an object having capacity to satisfy the desire of another cannot be had without difficulty, it is valuable, provided the person desiring it be of sufficient ability to pay for it. But if a commodity has no capacity to satisfy the desire of another, or if, having a capacity, the commodity can be had without difficulty, it has no value. A man living in the country may suddenly find the waters of his well dried up. To him, therefore, water has become exchangeable. Yet it may have no value because he can get it of his neighbor by a very slight personal effort. He goes to the city to live. Here he wants water as before, but he finds that he cannot get it, by simply going to his neighbor's well. He cannot get it by direct personal effort without going a considerable distance beyond the city. Rather than go so far, he is willing to pay some one for it in order to have it. Consequently the water paid for has value, because it could not be had without an effort,—without difficulty of attainment,—which the person had rather pay for than make directly himself.

Whenever an exchange actually takes place, price expresses or measures this difficulty. If I pay seventy-five dollars for a watch, the money expresses or represents the difficulty of attaining it,—in other words, the labor expended in making it; I had rather pay this money for the labor of another than make the watch myself. Whenever an exchange does not take place, difficulty of attainment is only another expression for the labor enhancing the exchangeability of an object. Yet labor does not always render an object more exchangeable. A man may build a house in the wilderness at vast expense, nevertheless it may have no exchangeability, because no one has such tastes and desires as the builder.

It is most important to remember when difficulty of attainment is used as an equivalent or measure of price, and when it is used as expressing simply the labor bestowed upon an object.

The second cause determining price is exchangeability. This we have previously defined as the capacity of an object to satisfy the desire of one who is not the owner. Now it is evident that whenever the desires of men change, the capacity of things to satisfy their desires changes also. Moreover, it is exceedingly difficult, indeed it is impossible, to find out all the causes which create and influence the desires of men. The causes are varied, often occult, unknown.

To A, a fine picture is worth $ 5,000 ; to B, not half that sum. Various reasons may be given for the different estimates of the picture. A perhaps, has a finer taste for art, or appreciation of the particular picture. He may think it will become more valuable with age, or that the genius of the artist will become more fully recognized in the future. The causes operating upon desires are too obscure often to be determined.

The paradoxical proposition has found defenders, that not only does price depend upon exchangeability, but that exchangeability depends upon price. This paradox does not, we think, exist; nor would it ever have been declared true, if the distinction between difficulty of attainment as an equivalent of price and as another expression for labor had been kept in view. Suppose a man is trying to find a house, with the intention of purchasing. After looking at several houses, he finds such an one as he wants. It is an expensive place; the grounds are laid out with great care and skill. It is the taste and labor displayed about the place that render it so exchangeable. Satisfied that it is the place he wants, he inquires the price. He has never thought of the price the owner would ask till now. Suppose the owner is unwilling to sell the house except at an enormous price which the other is unwilling to pay. The purchaser has the means to buy, but he is unwilling to pay so much. Perhaps he thinks the owner is trying to drive a sharp bargain with him. He turns away disappointed; afterwards he learns that the owner is willing to sell at a greatly reduced price. He purchases the house. Yet during all the time between the first examination of the house and the purchase of it, its exchangeability was unchanged. Hence it is clear that the exchangeability of objects is not affected by their price; but whether *exchanges actually take place or not*, these depend upon the price of the things exchanged. Take peaches, for example. When they are first brought to market, many say: "We will not buy now, we will wait till the price is lower." They want them in the beginning just as much as afterwards, perhaps more. Their exchangeability is the same from the first to the last of the peach season; though not many exchanges are made till prices fall to a certain point.

There are many rocks unseen when the waters are high, that appear when the waters recede. Yet the rocks are there, whether the waters are high or low. So with our desires. They are as real when prices are so high that no exchanges are made, as when prices are low and exchanges frequent. The only difference is, that when the prices of things rise above a certain point, the desires of men for them are unknown to the world; when prices fall below a certain point, the desires of men are found out through their efforts to gratify them.

There is one class of commodities, the exchangeability of which depends *primarily* upon their value. Remembering that utility is the capacity of an object to satisfy the desire of its possessor, we remark that some commodities have utility solely on account of their value. Thus a diamond is useful at the present time because it has capacity to satisfy desire. Let diamonds become plentiful, however, and not only would their value vanish, but their utility also. Nobody would want them. Now it may be properly said that those articles which are useful simply because they are valuable are only exchangeable for a like reason. But all other commodities are exchangeable because of the labor or other difficulty connected with them. This is the cause which renders them exchangeable. Yet the value of the diamond, so long as it has any, is measured or estimated by difficulty of attainment like other commodities.*

A third cause determining price is personal effort. This is one of the causes fixing the extremes of price. Thus suppose a purchaser is seeking for a chair. He goes into a store, and finding one that he likes, inquires the price. Being told that it is ten dollars, he remarks that he will not give so much, and that if the dealer will not sell it for nine dollars, he will make one himself. Personal effort, therefore, is the cause that fixes the highest price for the chair. As it is a cause determining the highest price of things, so likewise does it determine the lowest.

What do we mean by the highest and lowest price of a commodity? The first term is easily enough understood. The highest price is the most which a purchaser will pay for a thing. What is meant by the lowest price? The least that the dealer actually will sell for, and at which he must sell, else the purchaser will obtain the thing desired by a direct personal effort.

* This was the assertion really made by BASTIAT in his *Harmonies of Political Economy*, and which Professor CAIRNES has attacked. *Fort. Rev.*, vol. xiv, p. 424. But the error into which we think the latter has fallen is in considering the difficulty of attainment paid for as the difficulty expended by the finder of the diamond. This is only a partial consideration of the whole fact. The price paid for the diamond measures the difficulty of attainment which the purchaser had rather pay for than undertake himself. That is to say, the difficulty actually paid for is the one which the purchaser himself would probably have to overcome in order to find the diamond.

Willingness of deprivation is the fourth and last cause determining price. When vulcanized rubber goods were first made, they constituted a monopoly as long as the patent existed, so that no one could make them except the patentee and those whom he permitted. A, the purchaser, desires a pair of boots, but B, the monopolist, will not sell them for less than ten dollars. A's unwillingness to be without the boots leads him to give this price. But he would give no more. Either he would get them by personal effort (supposing that he could make them), or he would deprive himself of them rather than buy at a higher price. Thus we see that A's personal effort, or willingness of deprivation, determined the highest price which he would pay for the boots. The same causes may determine their lowest price. The monoply has expired. A wishes another pair. Now he tells B that he will not give him only four dollars a pair. Why not? Why is he willing to deprive himself of them if he cannot purchase at that price? Because he believes he can buy elsewhere for the price offered. Willingness of deprivation, therefore, is a cause determining price, for no exchange can take place unless the price comes within the limits which men will pay.

Moreover, willingness of deprivation cannot be resolved into any other cause of price. It is easily distinguished from exchangeability, for that quality may, as we have seen, inhere in an object after willingness of deprivation has prevented a transfer of the ownership thereof.

Let us now inquire when the highest and lowest prices are paid for things; and, also, what is the reasonable price towards which all things are tending.

First, whenever a commodity constitutes a monoply, then the highest price is paid for it.

Secondly, whenever the supply of a commodity is unlimited,—that is, when it can be produced without increase of cost,—then the lowest price is paid for it.

Thirdly, the reasonable price of a commodity is the cost of production, by which is meant the money paid for labor, material, etc., together with a reasonable sum for profits.

Let us test the correctness of these principles by applying them to actual exchanges.

Formerly, the screw part of the metal screw had a flat end, so that a hole had to be made in the wood previous to the insertion of the screw. In 1846, a screw was invented having a point like a gimlet, which could be inserted into pine and other soft woods, such as are most commonly used, without first making a hole. The great advantage of using this screw will be readily seen. It always fitted the wood snugly, and held the pieces secured by it firmly together, while it could be put in more quickly than the old-fashioned screw. Thus it had a greater utility, and likewise a greater exchangeability, than the other. Being a new and useful invention, the patentee had the exclusive right of making it for the succeeding eighteen years. By agreement with the patentee, a company was organized that began the manufacture and sale of these screws. The company fixed a price at which they were sold, which was not altered very much during the whole time the company had the exclusive right of making them. This company alone could make them, and they were not obliged to manufacture any at all; or, if they were, they could dictate the purchase price. Hence, it was in their power to sell at the very highest price people would pay rather than go without. They could fix a price so high that no one would buy them; they could lower it so that only a few would buy, or they could diminish it so low that many would purchase. The price, however, the company sought to fix was the highest price at which the screw would be generally sold in the place of the old-fashioned one. It was a comparatively easy matter to determine this, for they could tell by observation and inquiry whether these screws were used in the place of the old ones, and whether they were used where they should be, instead of something else in their place. And as the screws came into general use soon after their manufacture began, it was evident that the company had set as low a price as was necessary, in order to make extensive sales.

It is not always easy for the monopolist, in the beginning, to ascertain what is the highest price he can set upon his monopoly in order to reap the largest profit therefrom. For, be it remembered, the monopolist does not always seek to set a price at which the largest quantity can be sold, even though he should get a reasonable or great profit from his sales: but rather the highest price at which the largest quantity will be sold, and the greatest aggregate profits realized during the time he has the exclusive right of controlling his monopoly. Thus suppose the monopoly consists of the right to make and sell rubber goods. At first rubber boots are sold at eight dollars a pair. We will suppose that half of this sum is profit. Thinking that the sales will be largely increased by a reduction of price, the boots are afterwards sold for six dollars a pair. More purchasers are found at the latter price than at the former, but as the profits have been reduced one-half it is now necessary to sell twice as many goods as before, else the aggregate profits are diminished by the reduction of price. If, therefore, it is found upon trial that a diminution of price does not bring as large aggregate profits as the former price, then a higher price is set upon the goods. And as the monopolist can control the price of his monopoly, whatever it may consist of, so can he coldly squeeze out of men by trial the highest price they will pay for his things rather that not have them, without fear of losing his trade, or of being undersold, for there is no one to compete with him. This trial of the market in order to ascertain the best price at which goods can be sold, has been aptly termed by ADAM SMITH "the higgling and bargaining of the market."

We might have given a simpler illustration, showing how the monopolist can control the highest price of his monopoly. We will suppose him to be the owner of a fine picture by a celebrated master. It is the only one of the kind the master has ever produced. The owner offers it for sale at the highest price which he thinks any one is willing to pay. Suppose the price to be ten thousand dollars. A dozen men offer five, three offer seven, two offer eight, and one offers nine, thousand dollars for the picture. This is the highest price offered, and at which the owner must sell, if he sells at all. Having a monopoly, therefore, he is so situated that he can draw out the desires of men without losing his picture, and, consequently, can get the very highest price any one is willing to give.

Another form of monopoly may be mentioned, namely, distance from another market. Let us illustrate the character of this monopoly. On the line of the Chicago and St. Louis railroad lives a miller, who, at one time, sold a portion of his flour to his neighbors for eight dollars a barrel, and sent the rest to St. Louis, which, after payment of ten cents per barrel for freight, he sold for seven dollars. Hence, he received one dollar and ten cents more upon every barrel sold at home than upon each one sent to St. Louis. Yet it was cheaper for his neighbors to pay him eight dollars than go to St. Louis and buy the flour for six dollars and ninety cents a barrel.

ON THE MEANING AND CAUSES OF VALUE. 65

The extent of this monopoly may be easily enough ascertained. It is the difference between the merchant's time and expense of traveling to the market where the things are bought, and the time and expense of his customer. Thus, suppose that the expense of doing a retail business in New York and Chicago is the same, and that the merchants at both places intend to sell so as to clear the same net profits. The New York merchant buys a certain kind of silk of an importer and sells the same for three dollars a yard. Now, supposing that the Chicago merchant was amply repaid for the cost of transportation, traveling, etc., if he sold the same silk at three dollars and twenty-five cents per yard, yet if he actually sells it for three dollars and fifty cents a yard, the additional twenty-five cents in price is a monopoly which he enjoys in consequence of being so far away from the New York market.

The same principle may also be illustrated in the case of several kinds of labor. A noted artist is a monopolist. He may charge the highest price, and people will readily pay. So with a distinguished lawyer and physician. A WEBSTER or MOTT has the field to himself; he can make his own prices. So with some other men. But in proportion to the number of men exercising the same calling, and having the same skill, does the monopoly decline. Whenever labor constitutes a monopoly, its price is controlled by the laborer.

From what we have said, we think the reason clearly appears why every dealer seeks, so far as he can, to make the thing he sells a monopoly. For if he succeeds, he can get the highest price for it; while if he does not succeed, he can get only the lowest price, that is, a price which, if raised at all, the purchaser will not pay; for either he will acquire the thing by personal effort or obtain it from some other dealer. Let us restate this idea in other language. The dealer, if he be a monopolist, can get the difference between the lowest and highest price which a purchaser will pay for a thing; if he be not a monopolist, the purchaser saves the difference for himself. Is it strange, therefore, that every dealer should try to become a monopolist, seeing that he has this advantage, that he can get the highest price which the purchaser will pay for his monopoly? So we find all sorts of combinations among men in order to make monopolies out of their trades, products, and professions. This is especially noticeable of late among railways. They combine for various reasons; a prominent one being to control the price for carrying freight and passengers. And just here, in illustration of what we are saying, may be mentioned a monopoly enjoyed by Commodore VANDERBILT and his friends when the Erie Canal is closed. This is the only avenue for transportation between various places, except the New York Central Railroad. When, therefore, communication by way of the canal is stopped on account of ice, the owners of the railway have a monopoly, which they enjoy to the fullest extent. Mr. MILL gives a very interesting illustration of the way in which a monopoly was created. The Dutch East India Company at one time owned the Spice Islands, and could control the quantity of produce raised. In consequence of being able to limit the quantity, they "obtained a monopoly price for the produce" sold. "But to do so they were obliged, in good seasons, to destroy a portion of the crops. Had they persisted in selling all that they produced, they must have forced a market by reducing the price, so low, perhaps, that they would have received for the larger quantity a less total return than for the smaller; at least they showed that such was their opinion by destroying their surplus."*

We cannot stop longer to point out other forms of monopoly; some of them will come to light in connection with other parts of our subject. Besides, whether an article constitutes a monopoly or not, or whether men are seeking to make a monopoly of a particular thing or not, can generally be determined by slight observation. But this is true, that whenever a monopoly exists, whatever it may consist of, the monopolist, to the extent of his monopoly, can get the highest price for his commodities.

Let us take up the second principle, and test its correctness by applying it to other exchanges. Take the case of common cotton goods. They can be manufactured to an almost indefinite amount without increase of cost. But there is no monopolist to squeeze out the highest price which the purchaser will pay rather than go without them. In the case of the screws, the monopolist could get the highest price for them because he could control the quantity. He had one end of the string, and that the most important one, which no man could take away. Now, the situation is reversed. The purchaser can buy at the lowest price. If the dealer charged any more, the purchaser would go away with the expectation of purchasing of some one else.

And now the light breaks forth to clear up the darkness created by the monopolist. As his selfishness leads him to accumulate the largest aggregate profits from his monopoly, so do these high profits, by exciting the selfishness of other men, draw them into the production of the same things whenever it is possible. Thus, it often happens that if a business is exceedingly profitable, others will press into it until production becomes so great that the

* *Princ. of Polit. Econ.*, vol. 1, p. 552.

cost of producing will not be realized. One illustration will suffice. So long as the patent for making vulcanized rubber goods was in force, the owners of it realized great profits therefrom. Upon the death of the patent, so many rushed into the same business that the succeeding gains of the monopolist melted quickly away. So is it ever with monopolies. The selfishness of men which inspires them to create monopolies is counteracted by the selfishness of others, bringing about, sooner or later, their destruction. Hence, while one party in the industrial world is trying to build up monopolies, another party is equally zealous in tearing them down.

Having shown when the highest and the lowest price are paid for commodities, we shall take note of the reasonable price towards which all commodities are tending. This is the ultimate price which will be paid for all things. For no man will continue to produce permanently at a loss; indeed, he could not do so if he wished; as he would inevitably become a bankrupt. So Mr. MILL says: "Capitalists will not go on permanently producing at a loss. They not even go on producing at a profit less than they can live upon. Persons whose capital is already embarked, and cannot be easily extricated, will persevere for a considerable time without profit, and have been known to persevere even at a loss, in hopes of better times. But they will not do so indefinitely, or when there is nothing to indicate that times are likely to improve. No new capital will be invested in an employment, unless there be an expectation not only of some profit, but of a profit as great (regard being had to the degree of eligibility of the employment in other respects) as can be hoped for in any other occupation at that time and place. When such profit is evidently not to be had, if people do not actually withdraw their capital, they at least abstain from replacing it when consumed. The cost of production, together with the ordinary profit, may therefore be called the *necessary* price, or value, of all things made by labor and capital. Nobody willingly produces in the prospect of loss. Whoever does so, does it under a miscalculation, which he corrects as fast as he is able."*

Let us give one other illustration for the purpose of bringing into a single view the existence and operation of the foregoing principles. Several years ago checked woolen clothing was extensively worn, it then being fashionable. In the beginning, the quantity that could be obtained was quite limited, and as its exchangeability suddenly increased, it constituted a monopoly to a limited extent. The profit to the manufacturer being large, others began to make the same goods as soon as they could, so that the profits on them rapidly fell away to the cost of production. After a time fashion made a new decree that checks should no longer be worn. Immediately the exchangeability of the goods declined. Those who followed the decrees of fashion, if daring to trample so far upon her laws as to wear out what checked clothing they had, bought no more. True, some were unmindful of her dictates and were willing to wear checks still; to others these goods had always had a certain degree of exchangeability, and when the merchant was willing to sell at a price corresponding with their exchangeability to these purchasers, they were ready to buy. In the beginning, the manufacturer was a qualified monopolist, that is, he controlled the supply for a time, and so fixed the price; afterwards the exchangeability of the goods rapidly declined, so that the purchaser fixed the price; in the end, the quantity on hand having diminished, the final price was determined by the cost of production.

* *Princ. of Polit. Econ.*, vol. I, p. 555.

It is evident, therefore, that a reasonable price, which is the cost of production, will be the ultimate price of all things. This price will also equalize the division of gains so that no one will get more or less than he ought to have. It is beyond our space to show that the number of commodities bought and sold at a reasonable price are constantly increasing, yet the evidence of this fact is conclusive.

The difference between the highest and the lowest price of a commodity is often modified by various causes that we may call extrinsic. Thus a man may pay more for a thing, because of his friendship to the seller, or sympathy for his condition. People will pay more for things at fairs and festivals in order to aid the objects which such associations represent. So the members of a community may trade at a particular place, even though they pay a somewhat higher price for their goods, on account of the known character of the dealer for honesty, politeness, etc. Again, the desires of a purchaser may often be veiled, so that he does not actually pay as high a price as he would, if, his mind being like a piece of glass, the dealer could see what his real desires were. The same is also true of the dealer. These are seeming, not real exceptions to the principles set forth.

Having stated when the highest and the lowest price are paid, and also what will be the ultimate price of things, it may be necessary to say something further concerning the fluctuations of price. If, for instance, the price of wheat is one dollar per bushel to-day, and one dollar and a quarter to morrow, what has produced the change? Many would say it has been produced either because the quantity to be had has diminished or the quantity desired has increased. This is not always true. Suppose that three men are each desirous of purchasing a particular horse, and that each one is willing to give one hundred dollars for it, and no more. No greater price can be obtained for the horse because there are three customers than if there were only one.* The same is true in respect to many of the transactions of life. People will give a certain sum for a particular thing, and no more; no matter whether the quantity be more or less. The reason of this in many cases is, that if things cannot be purchased at a given price, others are purchased as substitutes therefor. Consequently, if the quantity of a commodity becomes much reduced, the dealer may be obliged to sell at the old price, or no one will buy. Remembering that personal effort and willingness of deprivation always fix the extremes of price, fluctuations in price are the consequences of a change in the exchangeability of things. So long as this is unchanged, whether the article itself becomes plentiful or scarce, its price remains the same. It is true when the quantity of a commodity diminishes, its exchangeability often increases, and *vice versa*. Suppose, for illustration, that the wheat crop is only half as great this year as last, so that all cannot have their wants supplied if they remain the same as before. I say to myself: "The wheat crop is short this year, but I mean to have all that I want, whether others get all they want or not." Others say the same thing. In such a case it becomes more exchangeable, so that all are willing to pay a higher price. Take another example. Not long since the price of laths in the New York market had advanced a little. What was the reason of this advance? It was suddenly found that the quantity on hand was quite limited, and the dealers believed that all the laths in the

* Mr. THORNTON has succeeded in showing that the law of supply and demand, at least as generally stated, is very defective; that if it were true, prices should often rise when they do not, and *vice versa*. (*Thornton on Labor*, chap. 1). Though succeeding in this, his attempts to replace it by the law of competition, we think Mr. MILL has shown to be a failure. See review of THORNTON's book by J. S. MILL, *Fort. Rev.*, vol. XI, pp. 505-518.

market, and more, would be needed at once to finish the buildings in process of construction. The dealers took advantage of this state of things to increase the price. They became in fact qualified monopolists, that is, they sought to control the price to a certain extent. When the condition of the market was found out by the builders, they rushed to the dealers to get their wants supplied in order to complete their work. The exchangeability of the laths suddenly increased,—the builders were willing to pay more for them,—and so the dealers could get the additional price they had fixed. Suppose the builders had met together and agreed not to pay the advance, but to send elsewhere for their supplies, would the advance have continued? Certainly not; it would have sunk down till the purchases were sufficient in number and quantity to satisfy the dealers. So it will be found in every case. Personal effort and willingness of deprivation fix the extremes of price, while the variations between them are dependent upon exchangeability, which in turn is affected by many causes, the chief of which is difficulty of attainment.

VI.

A MEASURE OF VALUE.

It is impossible, as we have seen, to find an invariable measure of value.

But a comparison of values may be made, showing what ought to be regarded as a real advance or decline in the value of a commodity. Suppose that the value of ten commodities have remained unchanged for twenty years, and after that time, one of them, wheat for example, cannot be exchanged for more than half the quantity of the other things as before. The value of wheat as measured by them, has declined in value, which decline may be regarded as a real diminution.

Although an invariable standard of value is impossible, neither is it needed for so many purposes as is generally supposed. A measure of value is not required to inventory one's possessions. Prof. FAWCET is wrong in saying that "without some such measure the amount either of a nation's or an individual's wealth could only be stated by enumerating a long catalogue of commodities. Instead of saying that a farmer is worth £9,000 we should be able to form no other estimate of his wealth, except by making an inventory of his possessions. The number of cows, horses, pigs, sheep, the quantity of corn, etc., he possessed, would all have to be separately enumerated."* Not so, for if there were no recognized standard of value, he could estimate the number of bushels of wheat or pounds of iron, to which all his property is equivalent. Instead of affirming that his property was worth £9,000, he might say it was worth 100,000 bushels of wheat or ten thousand tons of iron, or something else.

A measure of value is not required in making specific exchanges. For example, two horse-jockeys meet who wish to trade horses. Do they need any measure of value in order to swap animals? Listen to their conversation. A is willing to exchange equally, but B says no; he wants something more besides A's horse. "If," says the latter, "your horse is worth $100, mine is worth $200." In other words, B regards his horse as worth twice as much as A's. It is of no consequence how much A values his horse, or by what standard he values him, B regards his horse as worth twice as much. It will be readily seen that if gold or any other measure of value had never been thought of, the valuation of the respective horses could be as easily ascertained.

A measure of value is needed to compare or register the values of all articles of merchandise for purposes of general exchange. For, if one person was comparing the value of all things by wheat, and another by gold, and another by silver, and a fourth by copper, and so on, it would be quite impossible to have any general quotation of prices. As these are necessary for the transaction of business, as well as for estimating the cost of living, a standard of value is necessary.

Another need of a measure of value is to prevent undue gain or loss by persons in making contracts. For, if the measure be a

* *Man. of Polit. Econ.*, p. 301, 3d ed.

varying one and increases in value, the creditor will get too much; if the measure decreases in value, he will get too little.

In our country the unit of measure for expressing value is the dollar, which measure was established by act of Congress, April 2, 1792. This measure of value, which is a decimal one—consisting of a dollar and its fractional parts—so superior in convenience to every other measure in use, was the invention of JEFFERSON.

Although the unit of value-measure is the dollar, yet there are four different instruments expressing that unit.

The act of 1792 provided for the coinage of a SILVER dollar, of the value of a Spanish milled or pillar dollar, then current. The silver dollar was first coined in 1794, weighing 416 grains, of which $371\frac{1}{4}$ grains were pure silver, the fineness being 892.4 thousandths. The act of January 18, 1837, reduced the standard weight to $412\frac{1}{2}$ grains, but increased the fineness to 900 thousandths, the quantity of pure silver remaining $371\frac{1}{4}$ grains as before. The coinage of the silver dollar has been discontinued, except as a "trade dollar" for circulation in CHINA, JAPAN, and other oriental countries.*

The act of March 3, 1849, authorized the first coinage of GOLD dollars. They were issued the same year. They weigh twenty-five and eight-tenths grains, are nine-tenths fine, and contain 23,22 grains of pure gold. Under this act they have been coined ever since.

In 1862, Congress authorized the issue of a PAPER dollar, commonly known as the greenback. This has become the universal measure of value in this country. As this paper dollar is worth less than a gold one, people will buy and sell by the inferior

* Act of Congress, 1873.

measure. This is always the case. In proof of the fact it is only necessary to state that the prices of most commodities are largely increased because of the adoption of this paper measure. When gold or its equivalent was the only measure of value, in 1859, a barrel of flour was sold for five dollars.* When greenbacks were invented, in 1862, the same quality of flour sold in 1864 for ten dollars a barrel. Why this difference of price? Because in the latter case the flour is measured by greenbacks; in the former by gold. Some things are measured by the gold dollar now, the same as before the creation of legal-tender notes, especially importations, which are paid for in gold; the prices of almost everything else, however, are measured solely by paper dollars, because sellers expect to receive them in exchange for their commodities.

The last form of dollar is the BANK NOTE, which has the same value and characteristics as the legal-tender note, and the two are employed indifferently as a unit of measure.

Thus, the dollar—the unit of measure—embraces gold, silver, legal-tender- and bank-notes. If we inquire the price of anything, the answer usually is, so many dollars; or, if less than a dollar, the fractional part thereof. In store and shop, in railway car and manufactory, the price of everything is measured by dollars.

When a commodity is exchanged for a dollar, whatever may be the instrument expected in exchange, we do not have in view the receiving merely of some ideal thing, but rather of so much gold, or silver, or its equivalent. Some deny this. Says Mr. COL-WELL:* "When a barrel of flour is said to be worth five dollars, the party fixing that price does not mean the quantity of gold in a half-eagle, or of silver in five dollars. . . So, if in ENGLAND an article is said to be worth fifty-five shillings, neither party

* *Ways and Means of Payment*, p. 79.

forms any idea of the quantity of gold equivalent to that amount, although payment cannot be made in silver beyond forty shillings. So, during the Revolutionary war, when for many years there was only a paper circulation, prices were expressed in the various currencies of the different colonies, and very few indeed could have been guided by the quantity of gold or silver equivalent to any price expressed in their pounds, shillings, and pence.

"It is evident, therefore, that money of account is the medium in which prices are quoted and expressed in all countries. It is capable of measuring, comparing, and stating values to the utmost extent of the requirements of trade."

It is true when dollars are received and paid, we are not always thinking of the quantity of gold or silver they contain, but rather, what may be had for them. This is why it has been said that a counterfeit or base dollar performs equally well the offices of a good one, so long as no one knows that it is bad. Still, in receiving metallic dollars, we do not forget about their weight and purity. The reason why we do not always weigh them is that, from long experience, we find they are generally as heavy and as pure as the law requires. Let their debasement begin, either by the admixture of foreign metal, or by diminution in their legal quantity of gold or silver, and not a metallic dollar would be received without first being weighed. The same is true of paper dollars. As long as their future redemption is certain, they are readily received without thinking about the quantity of gold and silver that may be had for them; let their redemption become uncertain, and people will be disinclined to receive them, either in exchange for commodities, or in payment of debts. Their value diminishes, perhaps ceases.

It is true that an ideal money has been used by some people.

The famous illustration of MONTESQUIEU is always brought to the front by those maintaining the theory of an actual or possible ideal measure of value. The author of the *Spirit of Laws** observed that the blacks on the coast of AFRICA have a sign of value without money, purely ideal. A certain article is worth three macutes, another six, another ten macutes. This is the same as if they said simply three, six, ten. Dr. LIEBER once stated in an address before the Historical Society of New York, that "in Hamburg millions are exchanged in the name of the mark banco, but no such coin exists, nor is there any native coin of that commercial city—though, of course, foreign coins are in use." BARTH,† in his *Travels and Discoveries in North and Central Africa*, writes of a people who have "not at present any standard of money for buying and selling; for the ancient standard of the country, namely, the pound of copper has long since fallen into disuse, though the name 'rotl,' still remains. The 'gabaga,' or cotton strips which then became usual, have lately begun to be supplanted by the 'cowries' or 'kungona'. . . . Eight cowries or kungona are reckoned equal to one gabaga, and four gabaga, or two and thirty kungona, to one rotl." Here an ideal measure of value has survived the use of the real measure.

It is not true, however, that the dollar—our money of account —is ideal money, as Mr. COLWELL maintains, for we are thinking of its weight and purity whenever we receive it, or, if we receive a paper dollar, of its ultimate redemption in the precious metals. We admit that we are slowly approaching towards the use of ideal money in consequence of divorcing in thought the quantity of gold contained in the dollar from the dollar as a thing of pure imagin-

---

* Vol. 2, p. 59, new Am. ed.
† Vol. 2, p. 55.

ation. It is possible to have an ideal money.* The foregoing extract from BARTH proves this. That the time is not yet, nor soon will be, when our money will become purely ideal, is not worth time and space to refute.

Only one measure of value ought to exist in a State. For, the having of a second one is a source of confusion and loss. This has been clearly maintained by nearly all economic writers. Said Sir WILLIAM PETTY, as early as the seventeenth century, in alluding to the use of gold and silver as standards: "The relative value of gold and silver is modified according as human industry extracts more of one than of the other from the bowels of the earth. Consequently only one at a time should be used as money." And likewise LOCKE† has written that, "two metals, as gold and silver, cannot be the measure of commerce both together in any country: because the measure of commerce must be perpetually the same, invariable, and keeping the same proportion of value in all its parts. . . . One may as well make a measure, for example a yard, whose parts lengthen and shrink, as a measure of trade, of materials that have not always a settled, invariable, value to one another." MORAN and PATTERSON‡ are the only writers of late holding opposite views. They contend that if two or more things are used as standards of value, it is within the power of the government to declare what each is worth, so that no difficulty will arise from their use. This may be admitted, but the very instances MORAN§ has given of neglect and incompetence on the

* Money of account . . might exist, although there was no such thing as any substance, which could become an adequate and proportional equivalent for every commodity. *Sir James Stewart's Polit. Econ.*, vol 1, p. 526,¹ 4th ed.
"Civilized nations generally make use of ideal money only, because they have converted their real money into ideal."—MONTEQUIEU *Spirit of Laws*, vol. 2, p. 56.
† *Locke's Works*, vol. 5, p. 151, 2d ed., 1823.   ‡ *Econ. of Capital*, pp. 50–9.
§ *Money*, chap. IV.

part of the government, prove quite conclusively that it should not be intrusted with such a delicate duty. So long as one is sufficient for our purposes there is no necessity for having more.

The experience of FRANCE has led her to oppose a double standard. The French monetary commission, of 1869–70, consisting of twenty-three members, voted, by a large majority, in favor of a single gold standard, some of the members going still further, and insisting that it was desirable to ascertain the views of other countries, as to the measures required to carry out such an object.* Likewise the Belgian Monetary Commission, of November, 1873, reported in favor of adopting a similar standard, declaring that the rise of prices in their country had been greatly aggravated in intensity by the existence of a double standard. So the world is gravitating towards a single standard, and ultimately will have but one.

* See Corresp. in *Lond. Econ.*, Nov. 15, 1873.

VII.

MONEY AND ITS USES.

Great Mammon! Greatest god below the sky.—SPENSER.

The term money, taken in its strict etymological sense, means something standing between two extremes and relating them to each other. Money is exchanged for other things, but never for itself. Small boys, indeed, swap cents, but men use money as a medium to get other things than those parted with. Men have the same wants now as before the invention of money—they want bread, cloth, furniture, etc.—and money is used only as an easier means of satisfying these wants. If we could imagine a state of society in which commodities were exchanged without the use of money, we should readily learn the great advantage of having it. In such a state the various products of the earth were exchanged directly for each other. This system of exchange is called barter.*

* The following instance of exchange by means of barter is taken from a work upon *Fiji and the Fijians* by THOMAS WILLIAMS and JAMES CALVERT. They exchange pottery for masi, mats and yams. On one island, the men fish, and the women make pots for barter with people on the main. Their mode of exchange is very irregular; the islanders send to inform those on the main-land that they will meet them, on such a day, at the trading place,—a square near the coast paved for that purpose. The people of the continent bring yams, taro, bread, etc., to exchange for fish. . . The island tribes of the Great Fiji take yagona to the coast, receiving in exchange mats, mace, and fine salt. P. 72.

Of a time when this state of things existed HOMER sings:

> "From Lemnos isle a numerous fleet had come
> Freighted with wine. . . .
> . . . All the other Greeks
> Hastened to purchase, some with brass, and some
> With gleaming iron; some with hides,
> Cattle or slaves."*

Money is a measure of value and a medium of exchange. Having already shown for what purposes a measure of value is required, it now remains to point out the offices fulfilled by money as a medium of exchange.

First.—It is a labor-saving instrument. A, a hatter, desires a coat. He goes to B, a tailor, and making known his wants, offers to exchange a hat for the garment desired. But B says he does not want a hat. So A goes to some other tailor who makes the same reply; he remarks, however, that he does need a pair of shoes, and if A could supply him he would take them in exchange for a coat. A must now find a shoe-dealer, who will accept of a hat in exchange for a pair of shoes. After spending a great deal of time, A finally succeeds in exchanging a hat for a pair of shoes and then goes to the tailor and exchanges them for a coat. See how much labor might have been saved in this exchange by the use of money. A, instead of going to B, to exchange a hat for a coat, would have sold his hat for money to any one who wanted it, and with the money thus obtained he could have procured a coat. For A would have been willing to receive money in exchange for his merchandise inasmuch as he could exchange this for anything he desired. The hat could purchase only one particular thing, namely, shoes. Thus it had only a limited purchasing power, while money has a general purchasing power.

* Lord DERBY's trans.

Thus Prof. PERRY* correctly says, in pointing out the difference between money and other commodities: "They have the power of buying some sorts of things from some persons, it has the power, derived from the usages of society, to buy all sorts of things from all persons." Because money has this general purchasing power it saves a great deal of time in making exchanges. "At first view," says CHEVALIER,† "it might seem that the use of money complicated transactions, inasmuch as it necessitates two exchanges where otherwise there would be but one; but, in truth, its use is of enormous advantage, and we should take an immense step backward in civilization, if we were to return to barter. It has been wisely said that there is no machine which economises labor like money, and its adoption has been likened to the discovery of letters."

The utility of money as a labor-saving instrument may be strikingly illustrated from the experience of BARTH.‡ He tells us that in one of the villages through which he passed, the practice of the farmer was to bring his corn to the Monday market, but he would on no account receive shells in payment, and would rarely accept of a dollar; the person, therefore, who wished to buy corn, if he had only dollars, was first obliged to exchange them for shells; with these he must buy a "kulgu," or shirt, and with this he might succeed, after a good deal of bantering, in buying the farmer's corn. So great was the difficulty of getting things, in consequence of having no general medium of exchange, that often his servants would return from their purchases in a state of the utmost exhaustion.

Secondly.—It prevents the deterioration and loss of commodi-

* *Elements of Polit. Econ.*, p. 208.
† *On the Probable Fall in the Value of Gold*, p. 28.
‡ *Travels*, vol. 2, p. 51.

ties. C is a baker. He must dispose of his bread quickly after it is made or it will spoil. He cannot find only here and there a person who will give him any thing useful for it in exchange. Thus exchanges take place slowly and with difficulty, and while they are going on the bread becomes old and unfit for use. Long before disposing of his entire stock, a portion of it has been injured or destroyed. If money were in use, he could readily sell his bread for money, and with that obtain whatever he desired. By transmuting his perishable products into money, he may keep its power of purchase locked up in this form as long as he pleases.

Thirdly.—Money reduces the cost of a commodity. In a State having no money with which to make exchanges, more time is expended, perhaps, in exchanging things than was spent in producing them. Thus, the hatter previously mentioned might have consumed more time in exchanging a hat for the coat he wanted than was employed in making the hat. Consequently, the hatter is really deprived of the benefit of his labor, or the value of his product must be increased.

Fourthly.—Men do not always wish to exchange for equal amounts. A farmer who brings a fatted ox to market finds persons enough wanting a few pounds of beef, but none wanting the entire animal. He cannot divide the ox and give a part of it for a few pounds of coffee or tea; perhaps he does not want the value of one quarter of the animal in groceries or other things. By means of money all difficulties can be easily overcome. The farmer can first exchange the ox for money, and with that he can get whatever he desires.

Fifthly.—Money secures the employment of labor by providing for its reward. Without money how could a cotton factory, for example, be run with its hundreds of hands? The owner could pay them only in cloth; and what could be done with that? They certainly have not time to go far to exchange it for other products, and if they had, they would be unable to make the desired exchanges, for no entire community requires more than a limited amount of cloth. And if the operatives, in despair of getting their bread, should think of sending their cloth away, who wants it? where shall it be sent? A man having nothing except labor or skill to offer, might be unable to secure employment from those who wanted him and were willing to pay him most liberally, because they are not able to give him anything satisfactory in return; hence, he must labor for those who are willing to give, in ever so small quantity, the articles needed for his support. "The physician must take his pay in iron, or bread, or butcher's meat; and if any of his patients produced what he did not want, he must either attend them gratuitously, or they must die without assistance. Besides this, there are many products incapable of division. If a hundred men are engaged in building a ship or a house, how would they take their pay in kind, without taking the ship to pieces, and thus rendering their work wholly useless?"* Thus, without money the division of labor would hardly exist. Rather than lose the time to make exchanges or run the risk of losing the results of his labor, by injury or decay, or be subjected to the other difficulties mentioned, every man, so far as possible, would supply his own needs by direct effort.†

Besides, no man could perfect himself in any one art, trade, or profession. In the effort to supply his wants by making him-

---

* WAYLAND, *El. of Polit. Econ.*, p. 190. No author has illustrated the uses of money more clearly than President WAYLAND.

† BARTH says that he was repeatedly prevented from buying what he absolutely needed, corn, rice, etc., because he did not have, and could not get what the people wanted in exchange. *Travels*, vol. 1, p. 568; vol. 3, p. 203.

self whatever he desired, he could not attain to that perfection which is possible whenever man is permitted to practice a single art or trade, or make a single part of a complicated mechanism. Manufacturers could not thrive at all who sought to make those products requiring a minute subdivision of labor. But if the laborer be paid in an article that is universally desired, he can get whatever he likes; hence, it will make no difference in what business he is engaged as long as he can have money in exchange for his labor.

Such are some of the most obvious advantages of the use of a medium of exchange. To these, others might be added, but enough has been said to make it clear that money is of the greatest use as a medium for exchanging other commodities.

Money, then, combines these two qualities—it is a measure of value, and a medium of exchange. This definition is by no means exact, for the reason, not only that a perfect value-measure cannot be found, but also, that everything is a measure of value and a medium of exchange which is given or received for something else. If jack-knives are used as a means for getting other things, they are instruments of exchange and measures of value. Everything parted with is a measure of value for the thing received in each particular transaction. All that can be said of money is, that it is something used in a particular country or locality more generally than anything else for the purposes above stated. The mistake of writers upon this question is in trying to give a precise definition, which cannot be framed, unless it be exceedingly general.*

WILLIAM LATHAM has declared that coins, all notes, whether issued by the State or by banks which are endowed with the fac-

* See BANKER'S MAG., vol. 26, p. 545; article, "What is Money?"

ulty of closing contracts, paying debts and acquitting debtors, are money.* The defect in this definition is that not all of these instruments measure value, although all are mediums of exchange. A definition in the *North British Review*,† that money is "only another word for the machinery which accomplishes the exchange of commodities," is defective for the same reason. Prof. PRICE ‡ has said that "money is not an end but a means . . and thus we arrive at last, at the true view that money is a tool required for certain specific purposes."

Is it not a little singular that the uses of money, which are simply these two—a measure of value and a medium of exchange—should be the subject of so much confusion? For this, two reasons may be given.

First.—Many people believe that Government can create value and money. Government is as powerless to create value as ROBINSON CRUSOE was, when living on his lone island in the Pacific. Two persons are required to create value in every case. What people will take from the Government in exchange for what is given, lies as much within the power of the people to determine as of the Government. It has no more power of ordaining what its members shall receive from one another in satisfaction of debts than the birds of the air. Government may indeed, call a bit of gold "one dollar," but it is not the work or power of the Government which gives value to the gold. That is the product of labor which the Government never performed. Melt the gold so that every mark of the Government superscription is obliterated, yet its value is unchanged. The Government, by coining it, merely announces its weight and fineness.

Does the value of a piece of paper depend upon the inscription

* *Fort. Rev.*, vol. 4, p. 214.   † Vol. 35, p. 176.   ‡ *Principles of Currency*, pp. 166, 167.

of the Government thereon? A greenback has value. Is it valuable simply because the Government says so? Suppose the Government declared greenbacks to be valuable, and yet people declined to take them, would they retain their value? Of course not. They are valuable because the people believe that the Government will fulfill the promises of which these are the evidence.

Secondly.—Money was not designed to stimulate, but to facilitate exchanges. It was designed to save time and labor in making exchanges, but not to add to the number of them. Says JOHN STUART MILL: "It is a machine for doing quickly and commodiously what would be done, though less quickly and commodiously, without it."

This economic principle is very imperfectly understood else no cry would be heard for more paper money. The people, or a large portion of them, have seized the idea, that somehow the rapidity of exchanges, and the prosperity of business, depend upon the quantity of money in circulation; the greater the quantity, the more prosperous is business. This is a grievous error and arises from a total misconception of the uses of money. It sprang out of the fact that during the war, when more paper currency was issued, business vastly increased, and every one rejoiced over his prosperity. But the prosperity enjoyed at that time was due, not to an increase of currency, but to a greater demand for all sorts of products. The Government became an enormous consumer, and of course its demands were great. It was the National demand superadded to that existing before, which gave such an impetus to business. The currency afloat, or more strictly, partly afloat, did not affect the demand. If none had been issued the demand would have been as great. A coincidence was mistaken for a cause.

This principle, that currency was invented as a labor-saving instrument, to render exchanges more convenient, ought to be sounded in the ears of all who are seeking for an expansion of the present irredeemable currency. It requires no argument to prove that what people are really trying to get are the things which minister to the sustenance and happiness of life and body, and that money is merely a medium, a go-between, for getting them. Now, suppose there be an increase of money, how can these things be more easily acquired if their prices are increased? No one, for a moment, will contend that an increase of money does not tend to increase prices, and that any more can be purchased, in the aggregate, with the whole sum, than with the sum existing before the increase was added.

It is not the proper function of money to stimulate exchanges. This is a perversion of its use. It was intended to facilitate them and nothing more. Were this idea kept in view we should hear no more about an increase of the currency.

The Hebrews used silver as money, for it is written that "ABRAHAM weighed to EPHRON, the silver which he had named, in the audience of the sons of HETH, four hundred shekels of silver, current money with the merchant."* Among pastoral nations, cattle were frequently used, and still are, by some of the tribes of AFRICA. HOMER tells us that the armor of DIOMEDE cost nine oxen. Soon after the period of the Homeric poems, copper skewers were used as money throughout GREECE, which were superseded by the silver coinage of PHEIDON.†

---

* Gen., 23: 16.
† See RAWLINSON'S *Herodotus*. On the invention of coining and the earliest specimens of coined money, Book 1, appendix, note B. Also same work, Book 1, 94 and note 3; Book 4, 166, and notes; Book 7, 28 and 29, and notes. The Lydians, "so far as we have any knowledge, . . . were the first nation to introduce the use of gold and silver coin." Id., vol. 1, p. 180.

Once, the Anglo-Saxons regarded slaves as money; likewise, the people of NEWFOUNDLAND codfish in the last century. The Indians had their wampum; VIRGINIA, at one time, its tobacco; and MASSACHUSETTS, wheat. ADAM SMITH says, that in his day a village in SCOTLAND used nails. Among the Carthagenians an unknown substance enclosed in stamped leather was frequently used.* Likewise, bark stamped with the image of the sovereign in CHINA. Among the SPARTANS, iron passed as money; among the ROMANS copper, simple or compounded with other metals. Throughout the islands of the Eastern Ocean, and many parts of AFRICA and INDIA, shells are still used. The Æthiopians are said to have used carved pebbles. In THIBET, and in some parts of CHINA, small blocks of compressed tea serve as money. In some of the American colonies powder and shot were once employed; likewise, logwood in CAMPEACHY, sugar in the WEST INDIES and salt in ABYSSINIA. In some parts of AFRICA strips of cotton cloth are used. BARTH speaks of the use of the "rothl," an ideal money having no real existence, although pieces of metal of that name once circulated. He mentions the use of beads as money in many places.† An ideal money, called macutes, is mentioned by MONTESQUIEU, as once in use among some tribes in NORTHERN AFRICA. Sooner or later gold and silver have come to be regarded as money among all nations, which have been able to obtain them, either by industry, commerce, or conquest.‡

* Political economists and others have generally affirmed that the Carthagenians had leather money, but this is a mistake. See HEEREN's *Historical Researches. African Nations*, p. 68.
† For money in use in different parts of AFRICA see BARTH'S *Central Africa*, vol. 1, p. 568; vol. 2, pp. 55, 151; vol. 3, pp. 190, 230. Also BURTON'S *Lake Regions*, pp. 233, 271.
‡ MORAN mentions many things which have been used as money, p. 7; also SAY, *Polit. Econ.*, chap. 21, secs. 1 and 2. PATTERSON has well said: "We need not seek a definition in the intrinsic qualities of the substances out of which money is made, for there is not a single intrinsic quality which is common to them all. The generic quality which constitutes money is manifestly something extrinsic to those substances—some quality superimposed upon, or attributed to them, or at least to the shape which they assume as currency."—*Econ. o Capital*, p. 13.

The various things used as money differ greatly in value. Among highly civilized nations gold is the most valuable instrument. The reason is it can be exchanged among a greater number of persons than any other thing. It is held in high esteem by the people of nearly half the earth. Yet gold is not valuable everywhere. "If English merchants send out sovereigns to CHINA, the Chinese will not receive these coins as money—nor any other kind of gold coins. Gold is not money in the Celestial Empire; one-third of the human race (nearly one-half of the civilized population of the globe) refuse to accept the yellow metal as currency. Even in INDIA, where gold coins have been in use from the earliest times, the value of gold is greatly diminished."*

Why have gold and silver such a pre-eminence over other things as money? First, because of their portability. "One pound weight of gold will ordinarily command, in exchange, fifteen thousand pounds of wheat, thirty thousand pounds of Indian corn, five tons of rice, or a ton and a-half of cotton.† The same quality renders silver valuable as money, though less so, in many countries, because a larger quantity than gold has only the same value.

These metals are very valuable as money, because they are so malleable. They can be wrought into any shape, will receive and retain any impression, may be divided into the minutest quantities and again united, with the smallest possible loss. Hence, they are admirably adapted for coinage. In consequence of the small subdivisions into which they may be coined, they can be exchanged as of equal value for a great number of products.

* PATTERSON, id., p. 13.
† AMASA WALKER, *Science of Wealth*, p. 127, from which work the reasons why gold and silver are fitted to serve as money are chiefly drawn. See also SAY's *Polit. Econ.*, p. 170, 4th Am. ed.

They are of uniform quality. Found in CALIFORNIA, AUSTRALIA, or RUSSIA, gold is everywhere the same. The iron of different countries varies greatly. The copper of SIBERIA is better than that of GERMANY, while the copper of SWEDEN is better than that of SIBERIA, and the copper of JAPAN surpasses that of SWEDEN. It is not so with gold and silver.

They may be readily alloyed and refined. By alloy they are made harder, and so better adapted to use as money. Likewise, can they be easily restored to their original purity without loss.

They are unaffected by atmospheric influences. They do not rust or decay like iron, so that the gold and silver in the age of the PTOLEMIES may be in existence to-day, either as plate or money.

They are almost inconsumable by use. Nearly all other commodities are rapidly destroyed by using them. Articles of food and clothing, for example, disappear in a comparatively short period. Even iron, in the ways in which it is generally used—railroads, agriculture, the mechanic arts, etc.—lasts only a few years. But the duration of gold and silver is vastly longer. Investigations made at the United States Mint show that the wear of gold was only 1 to 2,400; that is, a gold dollar would wear out only by 2,400 years' service.

A transcendent reason why gold and silver are so valuable as money is their uniformity of value. The necessity of having commodities which will always possess value, and which will fluctuate as little as possible, is well understood. BURTON has illustrated this necessity in his *Lake Regions of Central Africa*.* At one of the villages which he visited, the value of money was liable to perpetual change, often, he says, causing severe loss to the

* P. 271; see BARTH's *Central Africa*, vol. 2, p. 55.

merchants who, after providing themselves with a large quantity of it (consisting of beads) find that it suddenly becomes unfashionable and consequently useless. I may promise to pay a thousand dollars in gold ten years hence, without running any risk that it will be more difficult to get than now. There is such abundance in the world, I would probably be able to get the money without paying any more for it than at the present time; whereas, if I promised to pay wheat, for instance, it might be very difficult to be had. The crop might be short, and if I was able to get it at all, I should be obliged to pay a heavy price. Or if, on the other hand, it was very plentiful, the person to whom I have agreed to deliver it would not get anything like an equivalent to that given to me. The need, therefore, of having something of as nearly unchangeable value as possible, is very great.

It is impossible to discover or invent anything, the value of which will be changeless. The value of gold and silver is variable, though the least so of any substances known. Consequently, as long as their value remains so uniform, they are exceedingly useful as money. One reason of this is, because they are so universally desired. Hence, if they have a greater value at one place than another, they instantly begin to flow towards that place where their value is smallest. In this way their value is kept steady.

To complete this side of our subject, we remark that gold and silver were valuable long before they came into use as money. That is a function superimposed upon these metals. This use increases their value, but it is not the sole or principal cause of their value; or the cause of imparting value to them in the first place. The Wampumpeag currency of the American Indians was regarded as beautiful by them, and so it passed as currency.

The same is true of gold and silver. They were prized before they came into use as money, else they never would have been used for that purpose. Being desirable apart from their use as money, they are found admirably fitted to serve this additional function, and so are used for this purpose.*

The inquiry may be pressed: Why did gold have value in the beginning? What gives value to anything? Exchangeability, which we have seen to be one of the causes of value, springs out of the manifold desires of man. Gold and silver gratified desire, the same as diamonds, pearls, or other things. When gold and diamonds were first placed in the canon of wealth, it is easy enough to see why they were such desirable forms of wealth to possess. A noble, we will suppose, has a large estate which he wishes to convert into some other form of wealth that may be easily transported. He intends to go a long distance. He cannot, of course, take his land with him, and it would be very difficult to take animals, or furniture, or any bulky merchandise. Besides, he might be robbed of these things on the way. But he converts all his land and cumbrous property into gold and diamonds which are a very small parcel, and that he can easily carry. There is less fear of robbers, for few, if any, know that he has these things in his possession. Again, his houses and lands are not so desirable, because they may be seized by his sovereign. A quar-

---

* "Gradually, in the course of time, and by the exigencies of society, they came to be appropriated by general consent to the uses of money, till at last that consent became universal in the civilized world. This appreciation was ulterior and consequent to the ascertainment of the many useful and admirable qualities of these metals for other purposes, without which there is no probability that they would have been employed as money. . . . Gold and silver are not valuable simply because they are money. This was not the original ground of their being held in such high esteem; but they have been adopted and have obtained universal consent to be used as money or a common medium of exchange because of their value for other uses, and because they are always in demand for such a vast variety of appropriations other than money."—COLTON'S *Public Economy.* See also on the Origin of Money; PATTERSON'S *Science of Finance,* p. 11; MILL'S *Polit. Econ.,* vol. 2, p. 19.

rel may spring up between them, and his domains may be invaded and laid waste. But if nearly all his property consists of gold and precious stones, he can conceal them from his destroyer by burying them in the earth, or by fleeing with them to a distant country.

Moreover, wealth was originally a sign of social rank, and is still a sign of power. When the lord lived near his broad acres, men knew what his rank was, from the fact that he was the owner of large possessions. Suppose he concludes to go into a country where he is not known. If without wealth of any sort, he is regarded as belonging to the common herd of mankind. But he comes wearing gold and diamonds and other marks of great wealth. At once he is taken to be a person of elevated social position, for one without such a position could not be the owner of so much wealth. In this respect, we have not yet passed much beyond the same rude state of civilization. Many people still wear gold and diamonds, because being wealth, they confer power, even if they do not rank. People look up to men of wealth in consequence of this; hence, many seek for those forms of wealth which may be easily displayed. They like the attention it draws. But let diamonds become as plentiful as the sands in which they are found, and who would wear them? If they were once prized because of their beauty, they are not so now, for let abundant mines be discovered and people would shake them off like the dust of the street. It is principally the idea to be considered wealthy, that leads men and women to wear so much wealth. Let a person who, whether wealthy or not, cares to make no display of it, and what does such an one think of diamonds? He does not wear them or care anything about them. This desire to display wealth is a scar of a barbarous civilization, which will disappear when wealth ceases to be a source of power, and intelligence and moral goodness are enthroned in its place.* It by no means follows that gold and diamonds will always constitute wealth because they are so regarded to-day. Yet, so long as they are, and so long as they can be obtained only by the expenditure of great labor, of course, a small quantity will have great value, and will remain very desirable forms of wealth.

The question has been discussed of late, how much money or currency does any country require to effect its exchanges. The answers generally given to this question display dense ignorance. They show how very imperfectly the functions of money are understood. It is looked upon by many as a mighty question which few, if any, are capable of answering. This is because such persons do not comprehend what the functions of money are. If they did, they would see that the question can be answered easily enough.

Whenever the business of a country has become adjusted to the currency employed in making its exchanges, whatever the amount may be, no increase thereof is ever required. This is one of the clearest principles of economic science. It makes no difference whether the volume of currency be great or small, prices will accommodate themselves to it; and if the amount thereafter be increased, other things remaining the same, the only effect of such increase will be to raise the price of commodities. So if a part of the currency be withdrawn, the effect is a depression of prices.

---

* COFFIN, in his *Our New Way Round the World*, thus speaks of the dress and ornaments of a Hindoo woman: "No Western lady can appear in such gorgeous costume, as the Hindoo woman before us, wearing a robe of crimson silk, reaching to the knees, trimmed with yellow bands across the shoulder, a yellow skirt edged around the bottom with cloth of silver, beneath which is an underskirt of purple silk. There is silver enough in the broad rings and bands clasping her ankles for a set of tablespoons, to say nothing of the display on her arms, round her neck, dangling from her ears and nose, and gleaming on her fingers, or of what she has lavished upon the garmentless child toddling by her side." P. 119.

It is of little consequence what the volume of currency may be with which a nation first begins to exchange its productions.

Now, as long as a nation sticks to the currency it has once adopted, and to which all values have been adjusted, there is no difficulty in effecting exchanges, provided that such a currency commands the perfect confidence of all. There will be no violent disturbance in exchanging commodities while the same currency is used on account of it. If exchanges are disturbed, they will arise from other causes than the currency. Like the sun, it will pursue its appointed course without interruption or change.

When a currency having the confidence of all is supplanted by an inferior currency, then exchanges are unsettled on account of it. Let it be remembered that no sound currency disturbs exchanges. If the currency employed by a country produces this effect, it is certain that such a currency is unsound. In the UNITED STATES we have driven out a sound, specie currency by means of an inferior, paper currency. While the former was in use, we were never troubled with the inquiry: How much of it does the country need? The currency was self-regulating; it was free from legislative regulation. But when it was supplanted by the present currency, exchanges were violently unsettled, and will remain so as long as it is below par. The more local a currency, the more violent are its fluctuations in value, while the converse of the proposition is equally true. Gold and silver have a wide circulation, and their value in all places is the same; but our paper currency has no circulation outside of our own country, hence its value is very unstable.

Keeping these facts in mind, it is easy enough to answer the question: How much of this paper currency does the country need? The less of it the better while it continues below par with gold. If it be an inferior currency, as it certainly is compared with gold and silver, we should not make it poorer by watering it, but rather contract the quantity and so improve its quality. The country needs no more of it; there is altogether too much now.

Besides, by increasing its quantity, its purchasing power is diminished, so that the aggregate purchasing power of the larger amount is no greater than that of the smaller sum. When an individual gives his notes for $100,000 and has only half that sum to pay them with, and his creditors know it, every one, except he be an inflationist, believes the debtor will neither improve nor sustain his credit by issuing more notes. The same is as true of the Government as of individuals. Its legal-tender notes are below par. The people prefer gold to them. By issuing more their value will diminish. There is no escape from this effect. The Government by no sort of ingenuity can increase the aggregate purchasing power of the currency as long as it is at a discount. By issuing more, its purchasing power is diminished, and the country has no larger amount in fact with which to make exchanges.

We conclude—first, there is too much currency now, and the excess will be felt so long as it is worth less than gold, which is promised in redemption of it; secondly, while its inferiority to gold continues, the question whether the country wants more of it or not is without any significance, because the country by no kind of legerdemain can actually get more if it be wanted. Of course a larger amount may be issued, but its value is entirely absorbed by the currency existing before.

When the currency of a country is sound, its value depends upon three things: first, the amount of business done there; secondly, the extent of its credit; thirdly, the rapidity with which its money circulates. If business is light, or money circulates rapidly, or credit be extensive, less money is needed than if the opposite conditions prevail, and so its value is less.

Money circulates more rapidly through the agency of banks than in any other way. By keeping money in these institutions they are able to loan it again and again; one person deposits a sum, it is discounted to another, he pays it into another bank, which, in turn, discounts it to some one else. Any report of the Comptroller shows this. The amount of the National circulation, according to his report for 1873, on the 12th of September, was $339,081,799, while the loans amounted to $940,233,304. Of course there was the legal-tender circulation of $356,000,000 besides; on the other hand, a large amount of currency was in the possession of the people. From these facts it is clear that currency circulates more actively through the agency of banks than through the action of individuals.

The use of credit in its various forms, bank checks, bills of exchange, etc., supply the place of money. We shall discuss hereafter the matter of the extension of credits in this country and how they operate to lessen the need for money. ENGLAND has not so much currency as FRANCE, though doing a vaster business, yet her exchanges are easily made by means of the various instruments of credit. In FRANCE, money is absorbed, hoarded; in ENGLAND, it is deposited in banks and kept in circulation. When the German indemnity was paid by FRANCE and new loans contracted, it was a world's wonder that such an immense throng should gather in Paris to subscribe for the loan. They came from all parts of FRANCE. It was the country, farming population. They had laid by money, and, instead of depositing it in banks, it had been kept in their houses. The loan being regarded safe, the money was drawn forth. The reflection is not creditable to that country that such a vast throng should be without confidence in the BANK OF FRANCE, or its branches; or rather, that FRANCE should have no money institution commanding the confidence of the people except the Government itself.

This fact, that credit serves the same purpose as money in liquidating debts, proves the necessity of maintaining it whenever possible, in order to avoid panics and the necessity of providing additional currency when they occur. For when these calamities arise and confidence or credit is gone, more currency will be required than at other times. Thus in the panic of 1873, everybody wanted money; no one dared to trust. Many at once came to the conclusion that the country needed more currency; that business had increased so enormously the present amount was inadequate to make exchanges. No one said this a week before the panic. Why not? Because, in fact, there was enough. So long as confidence was generally diffused there was no need of additional currency. The panic destroyed that, and then the demand for more money was universal. Upon the restoration of confidence, no more money was needed than before. This is the true explanation of the state of things which prevailed. When confidence was strong there was money enough; when confidence disappeared, more money was required to supply the place which confidence had filled.

VIII.

DECLINE IN THE VALUE OF GOLD AND SILVER.

Nearly all political economists agree that the value of gold and silver is depreciating. This depreciation arises chiefly from three causes: the larger supply; its lessening demand for ornamental use; and the substitution of other things for money.

In respect to the present supply, much labor has been expended to ascertain the production of gold and silver since the earliest times, yet no results thus far obtained command a very wide assent. In 1831, Mr. JACOB published an elaborate *Historical Inquiry into the Production and Consumption of the Precious Metals*, covering the field of investigation from the earliest ages to the time in which he wrote. This work, though abounding in wide research, is, after all, only an estimate, and that even very rude and imperfect in respect to the production of the precious metals during the earlier ages. Indeed, the difficulties of finding out the production and consumption of the precious metals, says M'CUL-LOCH, are "at least as great as their importance. They are not, in truth, of a kind to afford any certain conclusions, and we must be contented with those that seem to present, on the whole, the greatest amount of probability." For the production of gold and silver in AMERICA, from the discovery of the country to 1803, great reliance has been given to Baron HUMBOLDT's estimate in his *Political Essay upon the Kingdom of New Spain*, though Mr. DANSON,* who carefully studied HUMBOLDT's figures, together with the data pertaining to the subject, has found reason to amend them. CHEVALIER has carefully gone over the ground in his work upon the *Probable Fall in the Value of Gold*, though BLAKE's *Report upon the Precious Metals*, made to the United States Government in 1867, is the latest, and probably the best, exposition on the subject.†

The aggregate production of gold and silver to 1868, according to BLAKE's estimates, is as follows:

```
14 to 800....(Amounts supposed to be on hand)....$ 1,790,000,000
800 to 1492..................................      345,000,000
1492 to 1803.................................    5,820,700,000
1803 to 1848.................................    2,484,000,000
1848 to 1868.................................    3,571,000,000
                                                 ─────────────
          Grand total.........................  $14,010,700,000
```

From this amount the losses are to be deducted, which are as difficult to ascertain as the amount produced. Indeed, if possible, there is less agreement among writers in respect to the loss of gold, than to the amount now remaining.

As for the future supply it is well known that gold is derived from two sources—placers and veins. That found in the placers was originally contained in the rocks, which has been extracted by the grand operations of nature. Streams have rolled over them for unnumbered ages, breaking and grinding them to pieces, washing out the gold and carrying it along in their courses till it sank to the bottom. Placer-mining, therefore, is nothing but the

---

* *Journal of Statistical Society of London*, vol. 14.
† See also Commissioner WILSON's learned investigation in *Land Office Report*, 1867. His researches are very valuable.

digging over the beds of streams and rivers that have become dry, and in which gold is supposed to be deposited.

Once it was thought that, as the soil containing gold which had been thus extracted by nature from the rocks, was quite limited in extent, when it had been worked over, the future supply of gold would be exhausted. Such was the opinion expressed by the late Sir R. I. MURCHISON in his valuable work upon the *Siluria*. But now it is generally acknowledged that the normal supply of gold is to be derived from the rocks, and that the gold found in placers is only a small portion of the whole amount. This being so, it is clear that the future supply of gold depends upon the extent and productiveness of the gold-bearing rocks.

MURCHISON strongly maintained that the productive gold-veins were confined chiefly to the Silurian rocks, and that the quantity which they might yield would, not very long hence, be exhausted. The gold-bearing rocks in the Ural Mountains, in AUSTRALIA, and to a considerable extent, in CALIFORNIA, belong to the Silurian period. If "we cast our eyes to the countries watered by the Pactolus of OVID, to the Phrygia and Thrace of the Greeks, to the Alps and golden Tagus of the Romans, to the Bohemia of the Middle Ages, to tracts in BRITAIN which were worked in old times, and have either been long abandoned or are now scarcely at all productive, or to those chains in AMERICA and AUSTRALIA, which, previously unsearched, have in our times proved so rich;"* in all these lands gold has been imparted abundantly to only the Silurian or the associated eruptive rocks. Yet it has been conclusively proved since the time when the first edition of MURCHISON's *Siluria* was published, that gold abounds in rocks of every geological age. The explorations of TRASK and WHITNEY in CAL-

---

* MURCHISON's *Siluria*, p. 475, 3d ed.

IFORNIA in 1853 and 54; and, subsequently, the discovery of secondary fossils in the main belt of gold-bearing slates; together with the discoveries in HUNGARY in 1862,—prove that rocks belonging to the latest geological periods, even as late as the Tertiary, contain productive gold-bearing veins.*

Again, later geological investigation has shown that the quantity contained in the rocks, and which is accessible, is more abundant than geologists formerly supposed. MURCHISON maintained that the gold-veins parted as they descended into the rocks, till they became mere threads that could not be followed or worked to advantage. Mr. SELWYN, in his report to the English Government at AUSTRALIA in 1856 and 57, on the mining resources of the colony of VICTORIA, declared that there was no evidence from the mines in that place to sustain MURCHISON's position that any vein rich at the surface dies out or suddenly becomes unprofitable. It was true that the upper portion of many veins were once far richer than they are now. But the reason was very apparent. The gold had been removed by denudation. The very fact that many veins, even thus abraded, were still often very rich on their present surface, went far, in his opinion, to prove that the diminution of yield in depth, even though admitted to be true on a large scale, was still so slow as not to be appreciable within any depth to which ordinary mining operations might be carried. RAYMOND, in his report to the United States Government in 1870,† said that most of the gold-veins might be considered as practically inexhaustible in depth. Indeed, the statement of MURCHISON, according to this authority, "is completely overthrown by experience." Mr. J. ARTHUR PHILLIPS speaks the opinion now universally ac-

* See WHITNEY's *Geology* and review of same in *Sill. Jour.*, vol. 41, pp. 231 and 351, second series; *Sill. Jour.*, vol. 45, p. 334, second series.
† P. 457.

knowledged, that gold ledges are not more liable than ordinary metalliferous veins to become impoverished in depth.*

•Gold is found in almost every part of the world. The richest mine thus far discovered is the Morro Velho mine in BRAZIL. The gold region in RUSSIA has been constantly expanding by new discoveries, till it has reached to the Pacific. Indeed, the distribution of gold may be regarded as co-incident with the mountain chains of the globe. There is no extended region, no great political division of the globe, without its gold-field.† Quite recently, Mr. PUMPELLY‡ has published a work showing that gold deposits exist in almost every province of the CHINESE EMPIRE.

The production of silver in modern times was quite limited, till the discovery of the Comstock mine in NEVADA. Since 1862, about $80,000,000 have been extracted therefrom. Silver is very often found in connection with lead; and as lead veins expand largely as they descend from the surface of the earth, MURCHISON has declared that the lead mines will probably yield enormous quantities of silver for ages to come.

Now, if the gold and silver mines are capable of as rich yield in the future as in the past, the value of those metals will greatly

---

* " Recent observations and experience appear to lead to three important conclusions—first that the most productive gold-bearing rocks are by no means exclusively confined to the Silurian period; secondly, that aqueous agencies have been, and still are, actively at work in the formation of mineral deposits; and, thirdly, that gold ledges are not more liable than ordinary metalliferous veins to become impoverished in depth."—*The Mining and Metallurgy of Gold and Silver*, by J. ARTHUR PHILLIPS. R. BROUGH SMYTH, in his *Gold-Fields of Victoria*, maintains a similar view. He says, after examining two hundred veins, that " taking the whole of the information and results obtained into consideration, there is much reasonable evidence produced in support of the theory that quartz reefs are richer as they increase in depth, and in addition to this, that they are wider."

† BLAKE'S *Report*, p. 235.

‡ SMITHSONIAN *Contributions*, Oct., 1866. R. BROUGH SMYTH has written, in his work previously quoted, that the area of the Australian gold-fields yet unexplored, or imperfectly so, is vastly greater than any other upon the Pacific slope of NORTH AMERICA. Of the 20,000,000 acres of gold-fields in VICTORIA, not more than 600,000 acres have been explored, while many of the oldest mines are yielding, by improved methods, better results than ever before.

decline. It cannot be denied that the increased supply of gold has sensibly diminished its value several times in the history of the world.

During the period between the commencement of the Persian wars and the age of DEMOSTHENES, the precious metals became very plentiful in GREECE. Their value, consequently, greatly depreciated; as well, also, as in the time of CONSTANTINE the Great, who caused money to be coined from the precious articles found in the heathen temple.*

When JULIUS CÆSAR was emperor of Rome, he brought such masses of gold into the money market at Rome, according to MOMSEN,† that it fell in value, as compared with silver, about twenty-five per cent.

It is a clearly established fact that the value of gold has declined in civilized countries since the discovery of the gold mines in CALIFORNIA and AUSTRALIA.

Prof. JEVONS‡ asserts, with the utmost confidence, that there has been a rise of prices in ENGLAND to the extent of eighteen per cent., as measured by fifty chief commodities, since the year 1849. This rise of prices represents a real diminution in the general purchasing power of gold to that extent. Yet others, including Prof. CAIRNES, suppose the decline to be much greater, for the reason

---

* See BOECKH'S *Public Economy of the Athenians*, p. 14, Eng. translation.

† Vol. 4, p. 343. English transl., new ed. POLYBIUS says, that in his time the gold mines were so rich about [north of] Aquileia, but especially in the country of the Taurisci Norici, that if you dug but two feet below the surface, you found gold, and that the diggings (generally) were not deeper than fifteen feet; that in some instances the gold was found pure, in lumps, the size of a bean or a lupin, and which lost only one-eighth in smelting; in others it required more smelting, but was very profitable. Italians aiding the barbarians in the working for two months, gold became forthwith one-third cheaper over the whole of ITALY; and the Taurisci discovering this drove the associate Italians away and monopolized it themselves. At present all gold mines belong to the Romans. STRABO, book 4, chap. 6, sec. 12, quoted in MURCHISON'S *Siluria*, p. 475.

‡ *London Economist*, May, 1867.

that the course of prices previous to 1849, was decidedly downwards, so that the increased supply of gold prevented a greater decline of them, and also occasioned the rise above stated. In his volume of essays, published in 1873, he reaffirms his former opinions. He says: "all are agreed that within twenty years a substantial advance in general prices has taken place, the only difference of opinion is in respect to the causes of this change. Amongst economists I think it is pretty well agreed that the advance is, at least in large measure, due to the effects of the gold discoveries. But on the other hand, there is on the part of commercial writers, and in general of all who view the question from the stand-point of practical business, a strong disposition to ignore, or altogether to deny, the influence of this cause in determining the results." We are among those who think Prof. CAIRNES is right, that gold has declined in value, for the evidence in support of this conclusion will admit of no other explanation.

In this country the decline has been very marked since 1860. Elsewhere, we have compiled a table of prices showing what the decline has been in one hundred of the leading American products. Other things, in the production of which more labor has entered, the decline has been greater.

The decline in the value of these metals would have been still greater had not an immense quantity been drained off to the East. If A does not want a thing it is only a slight indication that it has no value; for B and C may want it, and if they do, of course it is valuable, although valueless to A. Hence, the precious metals, so long as they have a value among a considerable number of people, though not among all, their value will be preserved. Thus, silver, for instance, may become valueless among the most enlightened nations as between themselves, yet so long as such quantities of it are desired by the inhabitants of CHINA and INDIA as are at present, its value will not be materially lessened. For many years these countries have absorbed vast quantities of silver, else its value long ago would have declined. It is for this reason, says PATTERSON, that the prosperity of the world depends upon the continuance of this drain of bullion to the East."*

The value of gold and silver will decline from the increasing use of other things as substitutes for money. The use of bank notes, bank checks, bills of exchange, etc., as substitutes for gold in making exchanges has become universal. For example, the New York Clearing-House Association, representing sixty-one banks, received for the year ending September 30, 1872, checks, bills of exchange, etc., given by the several banks composing the association, $ 33,844,369,568. The use of this vast amount of substitutes in place of gold and silver has a direct influence in depreciating the value of these metals. Let an edict go forth that no such instruments could be used, or rather, supposing that all men were so corrupt that no one dared to use them, and the precious metals would enormously increase in value. Hence, it may be properly said that gold and silver are declining in value because credit or willingness to trust others has increased. It is one of the marks of an improving civilization. The substitution of the various instruments of credit for gold is attended with many evils, arising from unwillingness and inability to comply with their requirements; but as the infirmities of human character disappear, notes and promises of every kind will have general preference over gold and silver as instruments of exchange.

Gold and silver will decline in value as their use for ornament declines. Probably it was this use which first gave them

* See FAWCETT'S *Man. of Polit. Econ.*, p. 436.

value. Ornaments are worn for two reasons; one, to beautify the person; the other, to indicate rank and wealth. So long as gold, silver, and diamonds, are regarded as beautiful, they will be worn, for not less pains will be taken to adorn the person in the coming ages than in the past; but as indications of rank and power, they will one day cease to be worn, and with every declining use their value is diminished.

And, lastly, the value of gold and silver, and kindred forms of property, which depend largely upon the fact that much value is contained in a small space, will decline when other and more cumbrous forms of property become secure from seizure and intrusion. As society advances, and its laws become more clearly defined, more equable in their operation, and more surely and wisely executed, the desire to have property compressed into such forms that they may be quickly concealed, or transported with less danger of loss, will pass away. With this improved state of society, its members, instead of converting their wealth into the form of gold and diamonds, will build houses and enrich them with the works of genius and art—a tendency which is now clearly seen in this country and in EUROPE. Then, wealth will be displayed on canvas and in marble, instead of upon the body; in things that will minister not to the gratification of one man alone, and to him only for an hour, but to many persons and for centuries to come. In short, as the laws of property become more secure, it is evident that the forms which wealth assumes will be greatly changed. Thus gold and silver and the precious stones will be of little account, except as they may be useful in the arts.*

---

* One cause arresting the fall of gold is the increase of population; that is, population has kept up the demand.

We do not believe that gold and silver would circulate for a moment apart from their intrinsic value—that is, apart from their value as wealth, apart from their capacity to satisfy, immediately, human desires. We know some hold that the chief value of money to-day consists in its use as money, and this view we think contains much truth. Originally, it was regarded as wealth in almost all cases in which it was taken; whereas this earlier use has been superseded by another, namely, its capacity to bring us other things besides itself that we desire. But when it ceases to be wealth, it will cease to circulate at all. A merchant bought a certain kind of goods last spring, because, being fashionable then, they could be readily sold; but he declines to buy the same kind this spring, because, being unfashionable now, they do not command a ready sale. So it is with gold and silver. When they are no longer regarded as wealth, they will not circulate as money, for nobody will take or buy them. Everyone will be afraid to receive them lest they cannot be passed off. True, they have not changed in appearance or composition any more than the goods previously spoken of, but that makes no difference; man is omnipotent over his desires, and the fact that he wanted a thing yesterday will not rekindle the desire to-day. Hence, we cannot agree with those who hold that gold and silver will continue to circulate as money after they cease to be wealth: they may for a time, till people find out that their value is gone, just as a bad coin will circulate quite as well as a good one till people find out that it is bad. But when people do find out that gold is no longer wealth, it will not be wanted for any quality still inhering in it. Its value will irresistibly vanish, just as the value of everything else vanishes which is no longer desired. Gold and silver are subject to no peculiar laws by which they will remain buoyant in defiance of those laws which sink everything of a kindred nature to the bottom. Consequently, when gold and silver and diamonds cease to be wealth, and the world finds it out, they will become worthless.

Such are the principal reasons operating to depress the value of gold and silver, and which, it is evident, will continue to thus operate. Gold will multiply in quantity; the day of barbaric gold, of which MILTON disdainfully spoke, will surely pass away, while its departure is hastening by the use of substitutes for it, as money, as well as in other ways.

Two consequences flow from the loss of value accruing to gold and silver worthy of notice. First, those having it in their possession, or due them, will suffer loss. The loss of one class, however, will be the gain of another, and in this way there will be a partial evening up of the accounts between mankind. But Governments will be the greatest gainers. In this way, nearly all National indebtedness will be discharged, inasmuch as this is the thing which most of them have agreed to pay. Secondly, there will be a great saving of human labor in preparing an instrument to be thereafter used as money. PATTERSON has well put the question: "Is it not probable that some day . . future generations enjoying a more advanced civilization, will look back with pity on our barbarism in wasting so much wealth for the mere purpose of registering our wealth, and in employing such an infinitude of labor upon what could be accomplished without any." *

Little do we think of the sufferings and risk of life which poor humanity has endured to get possession of these shining metals. When the Californian mines were discovered, husbands forsook their wives, and brothers their sisters, the emigrant came from the

* *Econ. of Capital*, p. 10.

farthest shore, and all went and delved for the precious gold. They endured privation of hunger and thirst, laboring under the greatest exposure of body to disease and death—and simply to obtain these counters for making exchanges. The story of CALIFORNIA was repeated in AUSTRALIA. When that most auriferous country was discovered, thousands flocked thither to dig for gold. The Buckland river, where the largest nuggets were found, was literally a river of death. The rays of the sun, striking the rocks upon either side, reflected upon the faces of the miners, and caused a worse blindness than that which befel them before setting out for the diggings. A little way down the river was the cemetery where the miners were laid, so that every fresh miner was reminded of his probable fate, as he passed on his way to the mines. Nothing daunted, however, they hurried on to meet the fate of those who had gone before, and the multitude of graves remaining to this day testify of the magic and bewitching power of gold. Great as has been the acknowledged power of woman, cannot this dull metal claim a greater homage and devotion? But its sovereignty is to cease; all its long, painful history of conquests and sufferings is to pass away.

IX.

THE MONEY OF THE FUTURE.

We have not prepared this chapter with a view to setting forth any utopian or useless scheme, but to answer the assertion that gold and silver will continue to be used as money in the indefinite future, because there is nothing to put in their place. The necessity of money being universally admitted, and nothing having been discovered to supply the use of the precious metals for that purpose, the conclusion is drawn that they will be employed in that capacity always. Admitting the truth of the first premise, we deny the second, and of course the conclusion.

We have already shown that money performs a two-fold function; that it is a measure of value and a medium of exchange. In respect to the latter function, a representative of gold and silver in the form of paper currency excels the original in convenience. It can be more easily counted, transported, manufactured, is not so easily counterfeited, occupies less space, in short, it has every advantage over the precious metals as a medium of exchange.

We have adverted to the necessity of having a measure or standard of value, and the desirability of having this standard comprise the money of a country. It is not necessary, though, that the standard be a perfect medium of exchange. If a good substitute can be invented for this purpose, the standard of value may be a very inconvenient medium of exchange, if it were actually used as such, because there would be little need for transferring it in bulk. The chief requisite is to select the best measure of value, that is, a thing changing least in value, and which can be so represented as to form the best medium of exchange; in other words, so as to be most easily counted, carried, preserved from decay, counterfeiting, etc.

Another important feature in the medium of exchange we must not overlook, namely, that it be a representative of actual value; that the thing represented can be really had in exchange for the representative. In creating a currency or money for a country, it does not follow that an amount of money must always be kept on hand by an individual, equal to the representative in circulation, provided the issuer have ample property that may be converted into money. This is the principle upon which the National banks are chartered. Their circulation is secured, not by gold and silver in their vaults, but by bonds in the possession of the Government. So long as these are ample security for the payment of the circulation, no one will object to receiving the representatives of this property. In 1857, when all the banks in New York failed, that is, were unable to pay their notes in specie, no one objected to receiving their bills, because they were fully secured by State bonds held by the Comptroller of the State. The needful thing about the currency is to provide for its security. Now, since the representative of value is to be preferred to the thing possessing value, as a medium of exchange, provided the representative be fully secured, since the measure of value is rarely ever wanted so long as it can be obtained, it makes but little difference what sort of thing the security be as long as its value is unchanging. Hence, if gold and silver were displaced by iron, for instance, no one would be subjected to inconvenience or loss.

Does any one doubt this statement? What would be the effect of the change? A bank is created with a capital of 1,000,000 tons of iron. It deposits bonds which are deemed equivalent in value to the iron with the United States Treasurer, and receives a circulation for nine-tenths of the metal, that is, bank notes promising to pay all who take them iron in exchange. The notes of the bank circulate because they are secured by the bonds; it is of no consequence whether the bank has a pound of iron or not, for nobody wants any. All the bill-holders want to know is that their bills are fully secured; and so long as this is the case, they are content. Of course, a part of the security consists in having the property in which the bills are finally to be redeemed of as nearly a fixed value as anything can be. If, therefore, iron has as fixed a value as gold, it will answer just as well as a basis for money.

But one may say, iron is of various qualities. Very true, but that will cause no difficulty. The bank makes its notes payable in a particular quality of iron, and every other kind of iron might be graded by that. For example, the iron coming from the Iron Mountain in MISSOURI, we will say is taken as a standard. Rated by that, we will say that the iron of MICHIGAN is worth a quarter less or a quarter more, that the iron of NEW YORK is worth half as much, and so on. Every quality of iron in the world could be easily rated according to the standard, and every bank could make its notes payable in standard iron or other kinds, according to their value, measured by the iron of standard quality. As there is a great abundance of iron in the world, and as it must always be used, no trouble would ever arise in getting it to redeem any promises for which iron was pledged in payment. Iron has value for the same reasons as gold. The two are in the same category. If gold and silver become worthless so that they could not be used as money, there would be no difficulty in supplying their place, for the use of iron as a measure of value and paper as a representative for iron as a medium of exchange, would subject us to no inconvenience, and the world hardly know that a change had been made.

X.

THE GOOD AND EVIL OF BANKING.

Many advantages are derived from banking. These may be briefly mentioned. Banks are useful places for the deposit of money. They also collect it from all quarters in small and large sums from people having no use for it, and loan it to others who have. Another benefit is that they transmit, by means of drafts, money due in one part of the country to another, without sending gold or silver, or even bank notes in payment. In GILBART's *Practical Treatise on Banking** a number of advantages are recounted in addition to those mentioned, some of which seem quite curious in these latter days of conducting a banking business.

Evil also is blended with the good. Commercial and financial pánics, those disasters which are dreaded like war or pestilence, are one of the evils attending the banking system. Before the existence of banks these calamities were unknown. "What," says Prof. PRICE, "is this element, this distinguishing characteristic, of a modern crisis?" . . . The essence of the disorder is a phenomenon of banking. Without the banks there may be loss, there may be ruin, but there cannot be that pecu-

* Section II.

liar disorder which is popularly known by the name of a crisis or a panic. It is the commotion within the banking region which generates this specific malady."*

The panic of 1873 in the UNITED STATES is an exception. The banks did not originate it, nor were they a co-operating cause, unless the aid rendered to speculators may be regarded as aggravating the panic. The part they played in this disaster will be considered in a subsequent chapter.

As it is necessary to dissect to some extent the parts of a bank if we would know how panics are produced, we will begin first with its resources. Our attention shall be confined to three items.

First, is the capital of the bank which is invested largely in bonds and other securities. At present most of our banks of discount are organized under the National banking law, which requires the investment of their capital stock in the bonds of the National Government.

Secondly, may be mentioned the loans of the bank. These are made payable at various times, but generally within four months, rarely exceeding six, while many are payable in sixty days or even a shorter time. The funds loaned consist of bank notes issued by the lender, and deposits. Many people suppose that the greater portion of such loans are the notes of the lender, but this is a mistake. Thus, the return of the CHEMICAL NATIONAL BANK of New York City to the National Government for 1869 showed that its loans amounted to $3,956,415.06, but not a single bank note was its own. Its loans, therefore, were made from the $5,352,803.94† of deposits in the possession of the bank.

* *N. Brit. Rev.*, vol. 53, p. 235.
† The bank had $12,685 of its old notes as a State bank outstanding, but this is not worthy of mention in comparison with the discounts.

Take Sir John Lubbock's bank. He has given us the analysis of £19,000,000 paid into it; what does this analysis show?

Checks and bills	£18,395,000
Notes	487,000
Coin	118,000

Three per cent. only of the whole amount paid in consisted of bank notes, one-half of one per cent. was coin, while the remainder, ninety-six and a half per cent., was checks and bills. Deposits, consisting very largely of checks upon other banks, furnish the staple out of which the loans of banks are granted. Coin and bank notes are only small change. Again, to whom are loans made? Every bank has a number of persons, often a very large number, who usually are depositors as well as borrowers. They need loans to meet payments which are constantly falling due in business, and which must be discharged else the credit of the customer—merchant, contractor, whoever he may be—is destroyed. He relies upon the bank for assistance. The amount of assistance given is dependent, to a large extent, upon the amount of deposits the borrower may have there, and his ability to pay. In this way the custom is created by which the merchant confidently looks to his bank for pecuniary help to carry on his business, and likewise the bank looks to the merchant for the receipt and employment of its funds. This is a mutual benefit, for the merchant could not conduct his business so successfully, if at all, without the means thus obtained; and the bank would lose all profit on its notes and deposits if they were not employed.

Thirdly, the reserve. Under the State-bank system, the banks were required to hold a certain amount of specie with which the notes issued by them could be redeemed. Those transacting business under the National banking law are required to hold the legal-tender notes of the UNITED STATES in place of specie. The country banks must have a reserve of fifteen per cent. to redeem their circulation; and the banks in the larger cities twenty-five per cent.

Let us now cross over to the other side of the bank—its liabilities. These consist mainly of deposits, its own bank notes, and bank balances.

First, deposits are the various sums held by the bank belonging to its depositors. They are properly called *inscribed credits;* and are payable on demand. An inventory of them might show something like the following:

a. Checks drawn by the depositor, or others, upon other banks.

b. Notes of that bank, or of other banks.

c. Notes of individuals, or bills of exchange running to maturity which are deposited for collection, the amount of which is credited to the depositor when collected. Such notes and bills of exchange owe their existence largely to the sales of merchandise. "The sellers have received in payment, not money, but orders to receive money; and these orders they lodge with their bankers for collection."

d. Notes of the depositor, or of others belonging to him, which are discounted at the bank, and the amount thereof is passed to his credit. This is the origin of the greater part of all deposits.*

Though deposits arise in the several ways above mentioned, yet they are held by the banks upon very different conditions, either express or implied, which may be understood from the following classification:

---

* This analysis of deposits is but little more than a re-statement from AMASA WALKER'S *Science of Wealth.* See p. 148.

a. " Permanent or compulsory deposits made by business men wishing for bank accommodations, in order to secure larger loans."

b. " Fiduciary or trust deposits, made wholly for temporary safe keeping, by executors, guardians, treasurers of corporations, etc., who are receiving funds to be paid out, or invested at a future period."

c. " Active deposits, made by business men, to be withdrawn to meet current payments."*

Now, all of these deposits may be demanded at any moment. And herein consists the peculiar difficulty of banking. The loans are made for a fixed time, and the borrowers are paid either in the notes of the discounting bank, or of other banks, while the persons into whose hands these very funds may fall, can take them immediately to the banks issuing them, and demand instant payment thereof, either in specie or legal tenders, according to the tenor of the notes. In other words, the loans of banks are made payable in a given time, although the deposits and bank notes which furnish the basis for making loans are payable on call. How, then, it may be asked, can a bank ever make loans in safety? Simply because people do not demand their deposits as soon as made;† and because they do not demand specie or legal tenders in payment of bank notes as soon as they are received. It is true that depositors are constantly using a portion of their deposits; nevertheless, a large portion is left with the bank, which would remain unemployed unless loaned. That portion, which depositors thus suffer to remain for a longer or shorter

* WALKER, p. 149.
† Deposits circulate from owner to owner on an average once in three and a-half days, or 100 times in a year." GEORGE OPDYKE, "New View of the Currency Question." *Bank. Mag.*, vol. 13, p. 423.

time, is generally known. Besides, as depositors are, in many cases, borrowers, it is customary for them to have more or less upon deposit, in order to get necessary accommodations. "The permanent or compulsory deposits are not used at all by those who make them. They are made with the tacit understanding that they are to remain in the bank, and not to be drawn upon. They are made to secure favors from the bank, and in order to show a 'good account.' No bank, perhaps, compels its customers by any law or rule to do this; but custom in such case is as imperative as law. Banks are conducted wholly with reference to profit, and the most profitable accounts will secure the most liberal discounts. These deposits constitute a permanent loan to the banks, without interest; and the banks can loan the same to their customers on interest."* The custom determining the portion of discounts that shall be left with banks is variable. A correspondent, in 1857, wrote that the custom "very extensively" prevailed in the New York banks "of discounting large amounts of paper, with the express understanding or agreement that one-quarter or one-half shall lay in bank till another discount is obtained upon the same condition."† We may remark, by the way, that this custom looks very much like another mode of taking usury.

It is upon such deposits, and their own notes, that banks are able to make loans to individuals. For it is evident that if the banks could not ascertain, with any certainty, the amount of deposits that would probably be withdrawn in a given time, they could not loan any portion thereof. So, if their own notes were constantly returned for payment in specie, legal tenders, or whatever the law requires must be paid for them, the banks would

* WALKER, p 149.
  Bank. Mag., vol. 12, p. 470.

not dare to put any in circulation; indeed, it would be folly for them to make the attempt. But as every dollar of deposits may be instantly withdrawn, as there is no law or imperative custom to prevent this, and as there are occasions when this has been, or attempted to be, done, and which may arise again, consequently, banks are always occupying an exposed situation which the wisest foresight sometimes fails to protect. Moreover, when those occasions arise in which depositors generally demand their loans, the banks are least able to repay.

Secondly, another form of bank indebtedness consists of their own notes. Under the National banking act, the quantity that may be issued by any bank does not exceed ninety per cent. of its circulation. They are secured by United States bonds deposited with the Comptroller. As these bank notes are always redeemable in the circulation of the general Government, National banks are required to keep a certain quantity of it on hand in order to redeem their own notes when presented.

Lastly, we may mention bank balances. This form of indebtedness is worthy of notice, for we shall see hereafter that they have played a most important part in aggravating the evils of financial panics. They are deposits due from one bank to another. In August, 1857, the banks of the city of New York owed other banks nearly one hundred millions of dollars,* a part of which sum had been left with them to meet various liabilities, although the greater portion had been tempted thither by the payment of four to six per cent. interest.

Thus much is all that need be said upon the anatomy of a bank, in order to understand how it originates a financial crisis. To one familiar with the business of banking all that we have said was known before; to others it was indispensable.

* *Bank. Mag.*, vol. 12, p. 334.

How, then, does a bank bring about so dire a calamity as a financial crisis? It will be found, upon examination, that the banks have always produced them by withholding their customary loans; or, in other words, by withdrawing their confidence in the ability of their customers to pay. Thus, in the English panic of 1797, the BANK OF ENGLAND reduced its circulation—which, of course, was done by refusing to discount—from £16,017,510, on the 28th of February, 1795, to £8,640,250, on the 25th of February, 1797. Discounts were reduced nearly £2,000,000 between the 21st of January and the 25th of February of the latter year—the year the panic occurred.* "But even this gave no true idea of the curtailment of mercantile accommodation, for the private bankers were obliged, for their own security, to follow the example of the bank. In order to meet their payments persons were obliged to sell their stock of all descriptions at an enormous sacrifice." On the 25th of February it was felt that the fatal hour had come. The next day the bank began to increase its discounts, and the relief "produced at the instant" was very great. "After taking all the circumstances into consideration," says MACLEOD, "we cannot fail to acquiesce in the opinion expressed by so many eminent bankers and merchants at the time, by the subsequent avowal that experience had led many of the directors to repent of the policy they then pursued, and by the decided opinion of the Bullion Committee, that the policy pursued by the bank in this momentous crisis was erroneous, and that the severe restrictions they attempted to place upon commerce, very greatly contributed to bring on the calamity by which they were subsequently overwhelmed."†

* The exact reduction was £1,910,580. The first English panic occurred in 1793, and was produced by a similar cause.
† MACLEOD, *Theory and Pract. of Banking*, vol. 1, p. 401.

Again, in the English crisis of 1862, for six months previous to the event, the BANK OF ENGLAND had been "violently contracting its issues." This policy was continued till the night of Tuesday, the 13th of December, when the crisis was at its height. "During the previous forty-eight hours," said Mr. HUSKISSON, the president of the bank, "even the best Government securities could not, to any extent, be converted into money; other stock, of course, was still more unsalable; and Mr. BARING said that persons would not part with their *money* on any terms, nor for any security. The prevalent distrust, by invalidating the ordinary forms of commercial credit, had rendered a greater supply of money absolutely indispensable; yet the bank had been steadily doing its best to render money much scarcer than usual. At length it found that such measures were undermining its own position, and that, if continued for another day, they would involve the bank, as well as the country, in a common ruin. Accordingly, on Wednesday the 14th, the bank totally changed its policy, and discounted with the utmost profuseness. In the words of the deputy governor, 'they had (at length!) taken a firm and deliberate resolution to make common cause with the country.' Instead of refusing to discount, they *forced out* their money in loans in all directions. 'We lent it by every possible means,' said Mr. KEARMAN, ' and in modes we had never adopted before; . . . we were not on some occasions over-nice; seeing the dreadful state in which the public were, we rendered every assistance in our power.' " "This policy," says MACLEOD, "was crowned with the most complete success; *the panic was stayed almost immediately.* The mere sight of the bank notes was enough. 'At Norwich,' said Mr. RICHARDS, 'when the GURNEYS showed upon their counter so many feet of bank notes at such a thickness, it stopped the run in that part of the country.' By the 24th of December the panic was completely allayed all over the country, and by the end of the month the credit of the banking world was completely restored."*

The next great crisis was in 1847. The extreme pressure began on the 23d of September, when the BANK OF ENGLAND adopted more stringent measures to lessen discounts. On the 15th of October it refused to discount upon either Government stock or Exchequer bills as securities, consequently other banks hastened to sell their securities, and to hoard the notes received in payment. When the BANK OF ENGLAND failed to advance on good securities, they were sold for what they would fetch; so that the only effect of this narrow and restrictive policy was to create hoarding and panic. Things grew worse daily. Several large banks in Liverpool, Manchester, Newcastle, and other towns, stopped payment. The drain on the BANK OF ENGLAND became greater than ever. As the whole of the commercial world knew that the resources of its banking department were being rapidly exhausted, a complete panic seized them. A complete cessation of private discounts took place. No one would part with the money or notes in his possession. On the 23d of October the terrible game was played out. The Government, with the view "to restore confidence to the mercantile community,' . . recommended the bank directors *to enlarge the amount of their discounts and advances.*" What followed? The Government letter "was made public about one o'clock on Monday, the 25th, and no sooner was this done than the panic vanished like a dream. Mr. GURNEY stated that it produced its effects in ten minutes. No sooner was it known that notes *might* be had than the want for

---

* PATTERSON, *Economy of Capital*, p. 101; MACLEOD'S *Theo. and Pract. of Banking.*

them ceased." In the speech of the Chancellor of the Exchequer —Sir C. WOOD—on this subject, he said: "Parties of every description made application to us, with the observation, 'We do not want notes, but give us confidence.' They said, 'We have notes enough, but we have not confidence to use them; say you will stand by us, and we shall have all that we want; do anything, in short, that will give us confidence. If we think that we can get bank notes we shall not want them.' Parties said to me, 'Let us have notes; charge ten, twelve per cent. for them; we don't care what the rate of interest is. We don't mean, indeed, to take the notes, because we shall not want them; only *tell us that we can get them*, and this will at once restore confidence.'" Hence, PATTERSON says "that the restrictive policy of the BANK OF ENGLAND was the chief cause of this collapse of credit, aggravating a season of commercial difficulty into one of most destructive panic."* Had the bank continued its customary discounts this panic would not have occurred.

Let us turn to the financial history of our own country for evidence of the truth that the panics originating here were occasioned by the refusal of banks to grant the usual advances to their customers.

The financial crisis of 1817 continued two years. In July of the first-named year the directors of the UNITED STATES BANK determined to contract the loans of the institution. The bank in Philadelphia was ordered to reduce its discounts to the amount of $2,000,000, the same reduction to be made at the branch in Baltimore; $700,000 at the branch in Richmond, and $500,000 at the one in Norfolk. All of these reductions were required before the first of November. In the short space of three months and

* PATTERSON, p. 106.

ten days discounts had been reduced four millions and a half. This reduction had a very disastrous effect on the merchants, and through them on the rest of the community. Yet a still further reduction of discounts was ordered, till "the people were ruined;" then it was stopped. "For a time," says Gouge,* "the question in Market Street, Philadelphia, was, every morning, not who had broken the previous day, but who yet stood. In many parts of the country the distress was as great as it was in Philadelphia, and in others it was still more deplorable." "We heard," adds Mr. Niles,† "of a severe pressure on men in business, a general stagnation of trade, a large reduction in the price of staple articles. Real property is rapidly depreciating in its nominal value, and its rents or profits are exceedingly diminishing. Many highly respectable traders have become bankrupts, and it is agreed that many others must go as *the banks are refusing their customary accommodations;* confidence among merchants is shaken, and three per cent. per month is offered for the discount of promissory notes, which, a little while ago, were considered as good as 'old gold,' and whose makers have not since suffered any losses to render their notes less valuable than heretofore."‡

A committee appointed by the Legislature of the State of Pennsylvania to inquire into the causes of the panic got at the truth. They reported that the reduction of discounts made by the United States Bank, together with the reduction of discounts by the State banks, had brought about the commercial distress recently experienced.

Passing over the commercial crisis of 1837, which was caused by the United States Bank in the same way as the former one,

* Gouge. *Short Hist. of Paper Money*, p 32. † *Id.* ‡ Quoted by Gouge, p. 32.

we will take up the crisis of 1857. It was opened by the failure of the OHIO LIFE AND TRUST COMPANY for $2,311,268. Although many banks and individuals suffered by this loss, ordinarily, it would have extended no further. But the failure of a concern of such high commercial standing aroused the suspicion of the banks in respect to the insolvency of other corporations and houses. Their suspicion was confirmed soon after by the failure of the New York and Erie, and Michigan Southern, railroad companies, and other corporations whose stock and bonds had been considered solid investments. To aggravate the evil arising from these failures, a powerful combination of speculators in New York city devoted themselves to the unholy task of bringing certain large undertakings to ruin, and of undermining the National credit. Said a New York correspondent of an English newspaper: "A large body of active houses are known to be associated for the purpose; to influence the press to work out their views, and are alleged not merely to operate with a joint capital, but to hold regular meetings, and permanently retain legal advisers, whose chief vocation, it may be assumed, is to discover points that may enable the validity of each kind of security to be called in question, and thus to create universal distrust." *

The banks began to quake. They thought only of themselves. By refusing further discounts they stopped the issue of their own notes, and, as loans matured, they received their own circulation back again, or that of other banks, for which they could get specie, or their own notes by way of exchange through the Clearing-House. The loans of the New York city banks were contracted $25,000,000 between the 1st of August and the 24th of October.

* *London Times.* Sept. 10, 1857. See *Bank. Mag.*, vol. 12, p. 331.

The result might have been easily foreseen. The borrowers were dependent upon the banks for advances to meet many of their ordinary payments. They had been accustomed to rely upon the banks for funds; their business had been conducted upon the supposition that a certain amount of assistance from this source would, if needed, always be forthcoming. Now they suddenly found themselves cut off from the usual advances. Of course, those who had not the money, or could not get the means necessary to carry on their business, were obliged to fail.

When the evil consequences of a sudden contraction of loans is so apparent, why do banks pursue such an untoward course? For one of four reasons: First, to reduce their own circulation, so that when the crash comes they may be able to redeem the balance without difficulty. This may seem, at first sight, to be a dictate of prudence, but from the peculiar relation in which banks stand to their customers, it has always led to the most disastrous consequences, first to their customers and afterwards to themselves.

Secondly, another reason leading banks to decline discounts is distrust in the ability of their customers to pay. We have already seen that the panic of 1857 began with the failure of several prominent concerns of undoubted credit. The failure of these led banks to distrust others, and soon a general contraction of loans set in. One bank was frightened by the action of another, till the refusal to discount among them became general. Individuals followed in the wake of the banks, so that it was almost impossible to obtain loans from any source.

Thirdly, banks sometimes refuse to discount from lack of funds. We have already seen how largely dependent they are upon their depositors for loanable capital. This supply may become short at any time from three causes: In the first place, loans due a bank may not be paid at maturity, in which case it does not have funds to make new loans. This may happen by imprudent loaning in the first instance on the part of the bank, or the embarrassment or failure of a customer from circumstances that could not be easily foreseen. In either case the money due the bank is not forthcoming, so that it cannot be had to loan again. In the second place, the supply may become short from a sudden falling off in the amount of deposits. This may happen through the failure of the customers of the depositor, or diminution in the sale of goods, "such as occurs when trade is bad, and stocks of merchandise accumulate for want of purchasers, or when the harvest is deficient, or when cotton is scarce or dear, and the customers of cotton goods reduce their consumption."* In the third place, at such times depositors call more generally for their deposits.

Fourthly, it may happen "from a diminution of profits leaving a small margin for savings, and reducing the quantity of uninvested savings, which form a large portion of the means at the disposal of bankers."† In either case, the deposits fall away at the very time when the depositor generally seeks for extended accommodations.

The banks, however, before completely extinguishing the lives of their customers, lose their own also. When this is done, the panic is complete. Having now shown how banks begin a panic, let us follow it up to its consummation.

In attempting to take the lives of their customers, it is strange that banks have not seen that the former would defend themselves, and, if need be, destroy their foes in trying to make a successful defense. It is stranger still that banks have not seen

* Price, N. Brit. Rev., vol. 53, p. 241 † Id.

that their destruction was inevitable if customers were inclined to destroy these institutions.

How? By calling for deposits and specie. Both bank notes and deposits must be paid on call or the bank must fail. From this there is no escape.

Generally, banks fail from their inability to pay depositors. This, we think, is true in respect to English panics, without exception. It is quite as true in respect to the panics which have occurred here. As this hint has not been clearly understood among us, it is worthy of considerable notice. Very many have supposed that the banks have failed usually because they were not able to redeem their notes. Let us see what the truth is. It is clearly evident that there never is, nor can be, a run for gold apart from a run for deposits. "If the holders of notes," says PATTERSON, "who probably have not more than £5 or £10 on hand, lose faith in the bank, the depositors will still more surely take alarm. If a bank cannot pay its notes, how is it to pay its deposits? Hence, the common idea which attributes such panics to a real or supposed unsoundness of the note issues, is quite a mistake. There would be panics and runs on the bank, though they did not issue a single note. The demand for gold in exchange for notes is merely an accompaniment (and a comparatively trifling one) of the run for deposits. And such a run, if not promptly checked, must prove fatal; for no bank can pay up its deposits at once, whether in gold or notes." *

Take the panic of 1857. The merchants did not want specie, but loans. The banks refused to grant them. A large portion of the deposits they held were left to secure advances. When these were denied, did the banks suppose that such deposits would

From. of Capital. p. 95.

remain? Why should they be kept in the bank when all reasons for keeping them there had vanished? Besides, they were needed to make payments in order to continue the struggle a little longer with the contending elements. Perhaps, too, a spirit of retaliation quickened the determination of some depositors to withdraw their deposits. The language used by the New York city merchants to their bankers was this: "If you think yourselves justified, in a time of crisis, in bringing down scores of good firms, as solvent and reputable as yourselves, the public are still more justified in checkmating *you*, by requesting you to fulfill your promises to pay. Since it is on the plea of preserving the convertibility of the note *(which we had no thought of questioning)*, that you produced this wide-spread suffering, the outraged community may well turn round upon you and say, 'Very well, gentlemen, *let us see if you can do it.*'" The banks, of course, *could not do it,* and so they were obliged to close their doors. At the same time the Western banks called for their hundred millions of bank balances. It is true that in many places specie was demanded, but it was not distrust in the New York city banks to redeem their notes which led their holders to demand payment of them in specie. All of the notes were amply secured by the pledge of sound bonds held by the State Comptroller, besides the specie owned by the banks. And, in fact, every note was paid. Not a bank in New York city failed in 1857 having insufficient funds to pay every dollar of its circulation. Their notes circulated without loss of value during all the time that specie payments were suspended. "Even the worst crisis which ever befell the BANK OF ENGLAND—the crisis of 1825—so far from discrediting its notes, was actually relieved by the accidental discovery of a million of unburnt £1 notes. Commerce was probably never more severely tried than in 1847;

but the merchants, in their dread of the suspension of discounts, took to hoarding, not gold, but notes.* It was not convertibility of the bank note, as has been so often and so groundlessly asserted by Lord OVERSTONE and his compeers, that was felt to be endangered. Men feared that bills might cease to be discounted, or that the bank might be unable at the moment to pay cheques drawn against deposits."† True, some banks in 1857 were unable to pay their bill-holders in specie or anything else. A run on such banks would have taken place whenever their true condition was known; nevertheless, the run would have been as great among depositors, indeed greater, than among bill-holders for, if either class were secured, it was the latter.

We have thus dwelt upon this point, because, if a panic breaks out during the existence of the National bank system, it will be occasioned by a run, not for legal tenders in exchange for bank notes, but by a run for deposits. Assuming that the National bonds are a sound investment, and that they will be paid, no one will fear the non-payment of the circulation of the National banks, for it is amply secured. Let the banks fail ever so generally, their circulation will not aggravate a financial panic, for no one will lose any portion of it. If, therefore, the banks fail, the reason will simply be their inability to pay deposits when demanded.

We have now gone over the ground in respect to the cause of commercial and financial panics. We have seen that it is begun by the banks which, in destroying their customers, are in turn destroyed by them.

What are the remedies? The first remedy is that banks must

* This is what merchants and others did in the panic of 1873.
† *N. Brit. Rev.*, vol. 30, p. 183.

exercise care in making loans. How often have banks, imprudently, nay, even recklessly, loaned their resources? These may employed in the production of additional wealth, or, they may be employed unproductively. Whether they are employed in the one way or the other is determined principally by the banks. They are the power disposing of the uninvested savings of the nation, and deciding, mainly, to what purpose the surplus of corn and cattle, the profits of accumulated clothing and goods, the commodities and machinery of all kinds amassed, which constitute the national savings, shall be applied. If the resources of banks are employed unproductively, they may find it difficult, as they often do, in getting their funds. And if such loans are not discharged, according to agreement, the banks are deprived of part of their resources out of which future loans are granted and deposits are paid. "Everything," says Prof. PRICE, "depends upon the sagacity and prudence banks bring to bear on the loans they grant."

Profiting by the experience of the past, banks have loaned more carefully than formerly in respect to security. The comparison is immensely in favor of modern institutions over the old ones in making loans to sound parties and loans which are well secured. The National comptroller has said in one of his reports that a very thorough investigation made by skilled accountants into the value and condition of the assets of the banks proved that the bills and notes discounted were, to a remarkable extent, based upon *bona fide* transactions, while the accommodation loans were uniformly safe and well secured.

Another remedy proposed is to grant loans for a short time, but this would not obviate many of the financial embarrassments which occur, for in 1857 several of the wealthiest houses in New

York city failed to pay their paper which had only fifteen days to run. Indeed, it may be regarded as an open question whether the community does not suffer more by short accommodations than by longer ones.

Again, banks should be very slow in withholding their usual aid to their customers. It is true that no bank is justified in making a loan that will not probably be repaid. But it is the universal testimony of nearly all the observers of the various financial crises through which this country and ENGLAND have passed, that the banks have withheld their usual advances without cause. This was the opinion of the Bullion Committee of 1810, in respect to the English crises of 1793 and '97. The same is true in respect to the American crisis of 1819, when NEW YORK and all the Southern and Western States suspended specie payments. BOSTON continued to make discounts as before, though many regarded it as madness for her to do so. But the result was that she and all New England were saved from the loss which swept over the other States. In the crisis of 1857, a writer for the *Banker's Magazine* at that time, wrote that "the contraction of bank accommodations at New York, it is now conceded, was unnecessarily sudden and too great. . . . This course of contraction is now considered by our leading bank directors as unnecessary, and as productive of nearly all the evil that has arisen. A more liberal policy would have relieved the merchants, and thus would have saved the merchants extraordinary losses."* Indeed, many of them saw the end of their fatal policy, and made an effort to extend their loans; but, as all the banks would not agree to this, it was finally abandoned. Although the crisis was felt very severely in ENGLAND, yet its

* *Bank. Mag.*, vol. 12, p. 430.

worst effects were arrested by pursuing the opposite policy, namely, the expansion of loans. By this course the great American firm of PEABODY & COMPANY, which was known to be greatly embarrassed, though perfectly solvent, was saved. The English bankers had grown wise by their former experience, and, instead of withdrawing their confidence in the mercantile community when greater confidence was required, and when confidence was all that was necessary to save it, that confidence was freely given. Had the American bankers been as wise as their English compeers, the crisis on this side of the water would never have extended its ruffles across the ocean. The truth of this assertion is most clearly proven in the fact that the crisis began to subside as soon as discounts were renewed.

Another security against panics is the keeping of generous deposits. There is a decided tendency among banks to loan their deposits too closely. This arises from the fact that in New York and other places interest is allowed on them. This practice cannot be too strongly deprecated. Of course, in order to save themselves against loss, the banks are obliged to loan their deposits as quickly as possible, and ofttimes upon insufficient security, or to persons who will not employ them in a profitable manner. Moreover, an amount of capital is being sunk in railway and other enterprises at the present time, which is very lightly considered. In addition to this loss of capital, the industrial world is greatly disturbed, which has a marked tendency to cause a derangement of prices, and to require the withdrawal of a greater portion of bank deposits. With the cessation of labor comes a decline in the sale of goods, so that the merchant is unable to meet many of his payments, which he expected to meet from the sale of his products. He, therefore, has to look to the bank for more extensive accommodations. In short, it is safe to say, that in consequence of the greater competition in some kinds of business, and the diminution of profits therefrom, the depression and derangement in various trades and industries, and the loss of wealth in unprofitable investments—all these facts and indications should lead the banks to keep a larger portion of their deposits on hand, so that they may be able to meet new emergencies that may arise.

A last preventive of financial crises is co-operation. This may seem impracticable in our country, though it has been found feasible elsewhere. Thus, in SCOTLAND, in 1857, after the fall of the WESTERN BANK, the other banks having central establishments in Edinburgh, seeing that the panic was assuming a most destructive intensity, resolved to co-operate strenuously in the support of each other. "Accordingly," says PATTERSON,* "as fast as gold was withdrawn from the UNION BANK and deposited with some of the other establishments, it was immediately returned to the menaced bank. And thus on that critical 12th of November, there was a double current of gold passing up and down Bank street—anxious depositors carrying off their heavy bags in cabs, while steady bank clerks, with equal promptitude, carried back the bags to the UNION COMPANY. There was a dash of the humorous in the operation, but no measure could have been more beneficial alike to the banks and to the public. . . . Indeed, it is a curious fact that the greatest transfer of accounts from the UNION BANK, in 1857, was made to the BANK OF SCOTLAND, which is only distant some two hundred yards—the panic-stricken bearers of gold evidently being anxious to be rid of their

* *Economy of Capital*, p. 114.

precious burden as soon as possible, and depositing it accordingly with the nearest of the other banks."*

How marked the contrast between the action and wisdom of the Scotch banks and that displayed by the New York City banks in the crisis of 1857. When, for instance, the EAST RIVER BANK, on Saturday, the 14th of October, wanted only $ 20,000 in coin to sustain itself, and applied to several large banks for assistance, they refused to give it. Instead of making common cause with the weaker banks, the stronger ones seemed determined to break the others in order to retain their own presumed strength. They failed to comprehend their real situation—that the cause of the weaker banks was their own, and that by helping these they were strengthening themselves. Co-operation, therefore, among banks, is the true rule. They should profit by the wisdom of the Scotch banks, and by their own. They should remember that they stand upon a very thin crust which may at any time be easily broken through, and that the difference in thickness beneath one bank and another is not very great after all.

We think that there are some favoring circumstances to bank co-operation even in this country. Most of them are organized and doing business under the same system, so that in respect to their circulation all are similarly circumstanced. Besides this fact,

* "The proceeding, we need hardly remark, was perfectly legitimate. The banks to which the customers of the UNION BANK transferred their accounts became responsible for the sums thus deposited with them. That was a terminated transaction. The lending of the gold by these banks to their menaced comrade was a separate affair—amply justified alike by the solvency of the establishment to which the loan was made, and by the advantage which resulted from it to all the banks, as well as to the community at large. Such united action on the part of the Scotch banks, if timeously commenced, is adequate to stop the heaviest run for gold which any panic can occasion. To withdraw money in gold is a cumbrous and anxious process. One would require a cab to carry away even £1,000 in sovereigns. Moreover, no one is willing to run the risks attendant upon keeping a larger sum of gold in his house or office. And, hence, as happened in SCOTLAND, in 1857, money which is withdrawn from a bank, not for business purposes, but simply in consequence of distrust, is immediately deposited with another bank."
—PATTERSON.

there is another of great importance—that the banks grouped together in two or three of our large cities really determine the action of the rest. The banks located in each of these places can support one another quite as well as the Scotch banks, if they only will. And if they pursue this policy, rather than the unhappy one that has characterized them in the past—of each looking out only for itself—no doubt that banks in other places will be led to act in like manner, and thus co-operation be secured.

The foregoing was written before the panic of 1873.* The action taken by the banks then, and the splendid effects of co-operation, prove the truth of our observations, which are merely the deductions of previous experience.

* *Bank. Mag.*, vol. 26, p. 357.

XI.

THE FINANCIAL PANIC OF 1873.

A panic is a felicitous term for a disaster such as that which overtook the country in the autumn of 1873. Men were panic-stricken in respect to their money affairs, just as soldiers are sometimes panic-stricken in the presence of the enemy. They were frightened, and sold their property at ruinous rates; or did anything else according to the whim of the hour. Men noted for their coolness and deliberation, especially in time of severe trial, bent before the storm, lost their reason, acted like madmen, and sacrificed their property and reputation with scarce a thought of what they were doing. They ceased to be masters of themselves. The fortunes they had amassed were ruined, and many of the institutions they had built up according to the most approved manner, as it was supposed, perished as lucklessly as their managers.

What were the causes of these queer phenomena? For months the panic had been predicted. Shrewd observers could read unmistakable signs of its coming. In fact they were not very obscure.

An enormous amount of money had been invested in new railroad enterprises which do not pay, and will not for years to come. The Northern Pacific Railroad is a notable illustration. Running through an almost uninhabitable wild for the greater part of the way, and constructed thus far at great expense, it will cost, when completed, $100,000,000, and for twenty years, and perhaps longer, no dividends will be declared. Similar enterprises have been launched upon the country, in which an enormous amount of capital has been sunk. The country is poorer by every unprofitable railroad built. True, a portion of capital may be invested without the expectation of present gain, but no nation can afford to invest more than a small amount in this way. For the last six or seven years this country has greatly exceeded the limit. It has fixed more capital than it could withdraw from the floating mass without creating confusion and distress.

It may be asked, how was it possible to gather so much money for such foolhardy enterprises?

To begin with, the judgment of man is not always correct. OVEREND, GURNEY & CO. had a reputation next to the BANK OF ENGLAND for being careful and sound bankers, and immense sums were deposited with them; yet in six years they ran through their colossal capital and became bankrupts. The most careful will blunder. Undoubtedly, when JAY COOKE & CO. undertook to negotiate the Northern Pacific Railroad bonds, they thought the road would be a profitable enterprise. They were too sanguine. It is not fair to say that they swindled the public, for the heavy advances made by themselves are not consistent with the charge of fraud. The millions of their own property buried in this undertaking prove that, however defective their judgment, they at least were honest. The same may be said of other enterprises. Men are continually deceiving themselves. Engineers and contractors make mistakes in estimates and lead others into trouble.

Many a man supposed to be clear-headed and far-sighted is not so in fact. He may have been successful in business, and have amassed a large fortune through pure luck. The world judges by outside signs, for it can judge by no other, and when success is seen its possessor is forthwith credited with ability. A captain crosses the ocean fifty times and never meets with an accident; he has had fair weather all the time; on his fifty-first voyage he encounters a gale and is wrecked. When his ability is tested adequately he is found deficient, and thus with thousands of men in life. They have enough ability for all ordinary enterprises, or they may accomplish some great feat through luck; but when the construction of a great railway is undertaken, and gigantic plans are necessary, and wide and careful observation, the ability to thus plan and observe is wanting. Numerous projects have been floated upon the great names of Wall Street financiers, who are found to be as unsound in their heads as in their pockets, and grossly ignorant of the magnitude of their undertakings.

This truth cannot be driven home too deeply, that a great many have no ability commensurate with their reputation. They honestly suppose they have it, yet are mistaken. Deceiving themselves, they end in deceiving others. Of course, there is no sure way of distinguishing the truly sound and conservative men from those who merely appear so, but it is certain that people should have far less faith in the ability and ofttimes in the honesty of others, than they do have, and make more careful inquiry before entrusting them with money and other property.

Another reason why many persons have invested in miserable schemes is that they are intentionally deceived. It is a lamentable fact that men who have acquired an enviable reputation for honesty and ability sell out in order to make money. The story is often repeated. A manufacturer wins a great reputation for manufacturing splendid goods. They are wrought of the best material, and the work is performed by skillful hands. His goods are in demand everywhere. Having reached the summit of his reputation, he begins to manufacture goods of an inferior quality. He imposes upon the public. Just so do brokers and bankers impose upon the public. They are told that securities are perfectly sound, that the interest upon them will be promptly paid, when the negotiators know that the truth is exactly the opposite. Receiving a large commission for their negotiations, they allow that consideration to outweigh the ruin of their own reputations, and the loss to the deluded holders of such securities. They are willing to bear all the odium that will be heaped upon themselves for the sake of the reward they are to receive.

It would be a waste of time and space to recount the projects to which men who have achieved a fine reputation have lent it and ruined it for a reward. Often when oil, mining, and other speculative or bogus companies have been organized, some noted names are secured to head these organizations, upon whose reputation stocks are sold and innocent purchasers beguiled. Many are just beginning to open their eyes and find out how they have been duped by those in whom they had reposed the greatest confidence.

Another way in which the public have been beguiled into purchasing railway bonds is by being led to suppose the roads to be bonded less heavily, in proportion to their entire cost, than they are. Formerly, railroads were built principally by means of stock subscriptions, the bonds constituting much the smaller part of the capital invested. In those days bonds were safe investments. Now, the mode is reversed; bonds are sold for nearly the cost of constructing the road, and a little stock issued merely to center the control of the enterprise in a few persons.

So long as these bonds constituted only a small portion of the capital invested in railway enterprises, they were, in most cases, sound investments, and found a ready sale in the market. But, as we have just remarked, no sooner had railway bonds become popular with investors than the issuers took advantage of their high estimation to issue a larger amount of bonds per mile in proportion to the stock of a road than formerly. In other words, confidence in railway bonds having become strong, railroads have terribly abused that confidence and nearly destroyed it. Of late, issues have been made upon very inadequate security, and holders are likely to incur heavy losses.*

The last cause which we shall mention inducing the panic, was the inflation of the currency. Too much has been issued, and the natural result was imprudent investments. This is not the first time a plentiful supply of currency has led to unwise investing. MACAULAY has narrated the history of former rash investments arising from a similar cause. In 1688 there was an excessive supply of money in ENGLAND. "In the short space of four years a crowd of companies, every one of which confidently held out to subscribers the hope of immense gains, sprang into existence— the Insurance Company, the Paper Company, the Lutestring Company, the Pearl Fishery Company, the Glass Bottle Company, the Alum Company, the Blythe Coal Company, the Swordblade Company. There was a Tapestry Company, which would soon furnish pretty hangings for all the parlors of the middle class, and for all the bedchambers of the higher." A Copper Company

---

* See an excellent article in *The Nation*, entitled The Railroad Mania, in which the method of organizing a modern railroad and raising money to build it is succinctly given. Vol. 8, p. 185.

proposed to explore the mines of ENGLAND; a Diving Company undertook to bring up precious effects from shipwrecked vessels; and a Greenland Fishing Company could not fail to drive the Dutch whalers from the Northern Ocean. The same state of things prevailed when the South Sea Bubble broke. MACAULAY has described some of the companies formed a little before this time. "Wrecks to be fished for on the Irish Coast — Insurance of Horses and other Cattle—Insurances of Losses by Servants—To make Salt Water Fresh—For building of Hospitals for Bastard Children—For building of Ships against Pirates—For making of Oil from Sun-flower Seeds—For improving of Malt Liquors—For recovery of Seamen's Wages—For extracting of Silver from Lead —For the transmuting of Quicksilver into a malleable and fine Metal—For making of Iron with Pit-coal—For importing a large number of Jack Asses from Spain—For trading in Human Hair— For fatting of Hogs—For a Wheel of Perpetual Motion."

In these several ways, the public have been beguiled into investing very heavily in bonds and stocks that are of very little or no value. It is true that after many years, the lands along the line of these silent or lightly-traveled railroads will be taken up, and then they will pay. Long before that time the stocks and bonds will have been sold for a song, and some of those who first invested in them will have become bankrupt. Of course, so far as the circulating medium is concerned, it makes little difference whether it is paid out for profitable or unprofitable enterprises, for there is just the same amount in the one case as in the other. But one person can much better afford to throw away a part of his capital, or invest it where no immediate return is expected, than another. In fact, no person ought to invest in a hazardous enterprise, or one where dividends will be long deferred, any portion of his wealth, the want of which will cripple him in business or living, if returns should be long delayed.

It may be asked, where is the loss in such enterprises? The quantity of money in the country is the same, the laborers have had employment, and the rich have paid for it. Has anything taken place except a change of this money from the pockets of the rich to the poor? Is not this desirable? Something more has taken place. All the labor of the thousands of men thus engaged in unproductive employment has been thrown away. It is not the loss of money, but the loss of labor and capital. Suppose they had been employed productively in improving the highways and bridges of the UNITED STATES, for example, what a beautiful system of streets and highways would have existed over the land!

The waking up to the realization that many of the railroad stocks and bonds of the country were worthless or very poor property, coupled with the failure of some noted houses which had been aiding railway schemes, brought on the panic. When public confidence began to fail it were easy to depict the consequences that were sure to follow. For the panic took the same course as many of its predecessors, and it was not difficult to tell what was coming. The weakening of the prices of some stocks at once affected the value of the rest. The entire stock market at once became unsettled. Banks which had made enormous loans upon stock collaterals began to quake. They saw stocks going down below the margins, and they at once began to sacrifice their securities to save themselves. This was perfectly legitimate, and no one could complain; but when the market was deluged with great quantities, prices declined violently. Others became frightened and wanted to sell. In this way the utmost confusion was produced, prices grew low, and every one turned pale. To enhance the difficulty, many of the houses having large deposits payable on demand were called upon to respond. They were distrusted. Rightfully, too, for they had no money. It was all loaned to speculators, and could not be obtained. The banks could afford little help to any one outside of their customers, and their wants in many cases could not be supplied, for the banks were expecting a large withdrawal of deposits. Stocks continued to decline, and the difficulty was aggravated. There was no way of preventing it, for those having confidence in certain stocks, and who were desirous of purchasing them, had no money to buy. Thus the panic originated in a lack of confidence; first one was suspected, then another, and finally nearly all were. When confidence was broken down more money was needed to do business, and the sales of property at ruinous rates were made to get it. But so many wanted money there were no buyers, all were sellers. To suppose that $44,000,000 of legal tenders would have supplied the demand for money at this time betrays a great ignorance of the facts. A vast sum was needed because of the wholesale destruction of credit.

It is true the banks were not the originators of this panic, nor did they help it on, except in the way of loaning funds to speculators. When the crisis came the banks conducted their business admirably. Remembering their former experience—that in division all must fail—they united and weathered the storm which at first threatened to overwhelm them. Co-operation saved them; division would surely have caused their destruction.

XII.

THE RELATION OF BANKS TO SPECULATORS.

Speculation in wealth is not the production of wealth. If I borrow one hundred thousand dollars to buy stocks, and in three months they have risen, while in my possession, one-quarter of their original cost, I have produced nothing. I have added nothing to the nation's wealth. The stocks existed before I purchased them; they exist now without any additional value by any effort of mine. This cannot be denied. And the same affirmation is true in respect to anything that I may buy. If wheat, for instance, is purchased and held for a rise, which afterwards takes place, I have added nothing to production; I have performed no labor upon it to enhance its value. No greater quantity exists now than existed before. The whole business of speculation, therefore, is to be condemned because it is non-productive. To this principle there is no exception of a single commodity which may rightly form the subject of speculation. Whether speculation is in stocks, or in the daily necessaries of life, the principle remains the same.

Perhaps if we delay a moment upon the meaning of production, the truth of this principle may be more apparent. By production is meant the doing of anything to a commodity by which its value is increased. Thus, if A goes to Chicago and buys wheat and transports it to New York and sells it, he is a producer according to the above meaning of the term. He adds value to the wheat. Labor, or difficulty of attainment is one of the indispensable elements of value. Any man, therefore, who adds labor to a thing is a producer, provided his labor be desired or has value. The speculator never enhances the value of anything; or, if he does, it is not by means of labor, but by various practices and arts that are economically and morally wrong.

Hence, we repeat, that speculation is an unlawful calling, and is detrimental to every interest of society. The speculator adds nothing to the wealth of society; it would be as well off without as with him, so far as producing anything is concerned. In this respect he is only a blank. Yet if he had simply neutral qualities, society and commerce would have reason to rejoice. But he is the foe of every man who is engaged in production. He is the foe alike of the poorest man who toils for his daily bread, and the rich man who is obliged to purchase of him. Do you inquire how? By using the money that is required in production for purposes of speculation. The amount of wealth in the world is limited, and it is all needed in producing more wealth. It is required by the merchant, the contractor, the railroad, by thousands of men and corporations, to enable them to pay for labor and other things; in short, to carry on their business, and to add to the wealth of the world. Now, it is clear that all the wealth employed in speculation is withdrawn from other kinds of business. If money is loaned to a broker to buy stocks, it is diverted from the manufacturer, who needs it to pay for help, or to buy cotton. In order, therefore, for the manufacturer to get it, he must pay a higher rate of interest than would be paid if no money were diverted into speculative channels. The manufacturer, in turn, must sell his goods for a higher price, which is ultimately paid by the consumer, and thus the fact rises to the surface, that speculators are the foes alike of the rich and the poor, because they enhance prices by diverting from production the wealth that is needed for this purpose.

Speculation is to be condemned on two grounds: First, because it is a non-productive business; and, secondly, because it diverts wealth from productive business, thereby disturbing prices and adding to the burdens of society. But it is said that speculation is not always detrimental to the welfare of society. Thus, *The Nation*, in 1866, said that "speculation in gold (during the war) had certain beneficial results which outweighed its evils. It tended to keep gold in the country, by giving its holders the continual prospect of an advance, without which it would all have left the country in 1862, and have remained abroad until the close of the war, since it would have been quite useless here, and a mere dead-weight upon its holders. Abroad it would have drawn interest; here, it would not. The chances of speculation, however, seemed to promise something better than interest at foreign rates, and an immense amount of gold was kept here, to the obvious strengthening of the National credit; both the Government and the banks having always a handsome specie reserve. The very *excess* of speculation tended to produce this result, as it made shipments decidedly unprofitable, and foreign exchange unsalable. Thus we closed the war with a very respectable stock of gold, which then became available to the public at prices which were only too moderate."*

* *The Nation*, vol. 2, p. 809.

It may be fairly questioned whether "speculation in gold . . outweighed its evils." Prices were unsettled, causing greater loss and suffering. Any business that unsettles prices is, generally, to be condemned. One of the worst evils that can befall society is to have prices in an unsettled, fluctuating state. Thousands of people lose by a change in the price of merchandise. Yet this unsettled, disturbed state is brought about by speculation. Indeed, it is the state in which the speculator most delights to live. So long as the ocean of trade is calm, the speculator is like a ship with its sails uselessly suspended in the air; he does not move. On the other hand, the merchant, like a steamboat, passes over the surface of the untroubled waters, all the easier and steadier because there is no disturbing breeze. But when the wind springs up, then the speculator rejoices, for he can fill his sails and steer his vessel across the intended track of the trader, rendering his future more difficult and uncertain, by causing a derangement of prices, and by baffling the interests and prospects of trade. Not only were prices unsettled and capital diverted by speculation in gold, but industry and ability also. Thousands who were needed in other callings, forsook them to follow the bewitching life of a speculator. Or, if they continued in their former occupations, their minds were not chained to work as before. But is it true that speculation "tended to keep gold in the country?" If it did tend that way, then we have this curious and melancholy fact, that gold was more potent to the speculator for the purposes of speculation than to the trader for the purposes of exchange. Was this true? It may have been, but it is hard to believe that speculation competed so successfully with the regular demands of commerce, that it became the omnipotent master of the universally recognized instrument of exchange. But if it did

—if gold was kept in the country by speculation, was it "to the obvious strengthening of the National credit?" Certainly, not all the gold in the country belonged to the National Government, and the portion not so owned, could have had very little influence in the "strengthening of the National credit." And if we owed debts abroad which only gold could discharge, was the National credit more strengthened by the existence of such a strong spirit of speculation that gold was tempted to remain here as an instrument of speculation, than the National credit would have been strengthened if the gold had been sent away to discharge that indebtedness?

The Nation also alludes to speculation in food, that it "is often censured with special severity. Yet," it says, "there is nothing in which it is more plainly beneficial. Were it not for speculators, the farmers would be utterly unable to sell plentiful crops, while the price paid by consumers would be so low as to lead to extreme wastefulness. When in the course of nature a barren season came round, there would be no stores laid up against it, and all the desolations of famine would follow. JOSEPH and PHARAOH were, perhaps, the greatest speculators on record; and what is clearer than that their speculation in corn was the salvation of EGYPT?" Now we apprehend that the defect in this mode of reasoning is, that the business of an exchanger who is a producer, is confounded with that of a speculator. A man, it is true, may purchase for the sake of the reasonable gains to which he is entitled, and for nothing more; he is then only a producer. But he may also purchase with the expectation of an additional rise which may take place, from the simple fact that by purchasing all the wheat in the country, for instance, its price may be controlled. What we condemn is, the purchase of the wheat for this latter purpose. Supposing that it was not purchased for this end, is it true that "the farmers would be utterly unable to sell plentiful crops?" If wheat is needed, will it not be purchased by the regular producer, merchant, or exchanger, even though a speculator is unknown? The writer says, "Were it not for speculators, the farmers would be utterly unable to sell plentiful crops." Is this true? Would the merchant fold his arms and stop his ears so that he could not hear the demands of his customers, while the granaries of the farmers were filled to bursting? Would he forego the reasonable profits that could be made on the purchase and sale of wheat to his customers, if unable to reap the gains of the speculator? Such is the effect of *The Nation's* argument, and yet we see that it is all knocked over by the latter part of the very sentence just quoted. For he adds: "The price paid by consumers would be so low as to lead to extreme wastefulness." But he had previously said that "the farmers would be utterly unable to sell plentiful crops were it not for the speculators." Is it possible to harmonize these statements? If "the price paid by consumers would be so low as to lead to extreme wastefulness, were it not for speculators," then evidently, the people could obtain the crops without the speculators, for they could not waste what they did not have, and, of course, *the farmers would be able to sell their crops.* Nor do the farmers get any more for their produce by selling it to the speculators, ordinarily, than they would get if they sold directly to the wholesale or retail merchants or their consumers.

In regard to the husbanding of stores for periods of scarcity, there is no speculation in this. We have said that speculation consists in obtaining control of the supply of a thing, so that the price thereof can be fixed by the holder with the intention of selling at more than a reasonable profit. But JOSEPH and PHARAOH were not speculators, because, apprehending a famine, they provided against it by storing up an extraordinary quantity of provisions. There is no speculation, necessarily, in the purchase of a large quantity, but only when the owner takes advantage of the fact to charge an extraordinary and wrongful price for the same. Consequently, JOSEPH and PHARAOH were not speculators, unless they sold at such a price; and if we remember correctly, there is no proof that they did. It may be that with these explanations there would be no contrariety between the writer of the article above alluded to and ourselves; that the difference has arisen in consequence of not developing the subject as fully as we have done.

We believe the rule of pure morality requires that only a reasonable profit be sought upon any kind of product. What such a profit is depends upon circumstances. If a business involves a tremendous risk, a reasonable charge is greater than in a business unaccompanied with risk. Thus the fruit-dealer is justified in charging more for his fruit which is perishable, than a wheat-dealer for wheat which will keep. When the Atlantic cable was laid and put in successful working, the company was justified in charging more on account of the greater risk, and to get back the money sunk in previous unsuccessful attempts. But advantages are not to be taken of the scarcity of the market to force up prices, much less to make the market scarce by buying all the goods of a particular kind that are likely to be in demand. When prices are sought to be influenced by any unfair means, there is no excuse for loaning money to help on the movement. Every one knows that railroad stocks are worth, generally speaking, quite as much one day as another; yet their prices are always fluctuating, and a great many buy, hoping to gain by these changes. They are caused, generally, by unfair means, by the meanest stories and canards. It is an immoral business to purchase stocks for speculative purposes, or to loan money to those who wish to do so. Banks have no right to help speculators of any kind.

It may be asked, what business has a bank to inquire of its customer what he proposes to do with his loan? It is sometimes the duty of a bank to make such inquiry. Should a banker suspect that an applicant wanted a loan of a thousand dollars in ten one-hundred-dollar bills for the purpose of counterfeiting them, he would not have the right to make, nor would he make such a loan. Neither is it right for a bank to make a loan which is to be used in payment for real estate.

Formerly, it was the custom of banks to assist only those who were engaged in productive occupations—merchants, manufacturers, and the like. We admit this custom has been thrown away and another adopted, namely, that he who pays best shall be first accommodated, without considering or caring to what use the money is to be applied. Instead of telling the borrower that he must engage in some productive business if he wishes to have assistance from the bank, the only thing apparently thought of is the rate of interest and the security. If the most unprincipled speculator in Wall Street pays a good rate of interest, and furnishes good security, the bank makes no further inquiry.

Banking capital is designed to aid men in business, to facilitate exchanges, in paying for labor, goods, and the like, and not in erecting buildings, paying for real estate, or helping speculators. Fixed capital should come from individuals and savings institutions, not from banks of discount; hence, every application to a bank of discount for a loan for either of these latter purposes should be at once declined.

Besides, a National bank has no right, according to law, to do this. It is wrong not only in an economic and moral point of view, but it is contrary to the spirit and intent of the National bank act, under which most of our banks live and do business. A government official* has rightly said that "a charter to carry on the business of banking does not give power to buy or sell real estate, to ship goods to a foreign port, *or to engage in or promote any speculative* operation."

It cannot be denied that our banks, especially in the larger cities, assist speculators to an enormous extent.† Thus we find in the United States Comptroller's report for 1868, that "the bank statements of New York, taken separately," show the loans of the banks in that State to have been substantially as follows:

Commercial or business paper	$90,000,000
Demand loans	68,500,000
Accommodation loans	3,500,000
Suspended loans	1,500,000
Total	$163,500,000

Nine-sixteenths of these loans are legitimate business paper; "the amount loaned on call for commercial purposes is not stated, but reliable information leads to the belief that it is very small." Merchants cannot use to advantage money payable on call, as the goods which they buy with it cannot be instantly converted into cash. But stock and gold speculators can almost

---

* United States Comptroller of the Currency, report of 1869

† The only notable refusal of banks to loan speculators is that of the Western banks to the grain speculators in the summer of 1870.—*The Nation*, vol. 10, p. 416.

always realize on these forms of property very quickly, so that they are able to use money payable on call with profit. Hence the United States Comptroller has drawn the inference, "that nearly one-half of the available resources of the National banks in the City of New York are used in the operations of the stock and gold exchange."

"In addition to this direct loan of $70,000,000, they furnish facilities by means of certified checks to the same class of operators, ranging from $110,000,000 to $120,000,000 daily (on the 5th of October the amount was $112,800,000). Taking the call loans and the certified checks together, the somewhat startling fact is developed, that the New York National banks furnish $70,000,000 of capital and $112,000,000 of credit for speculation, or one hundred and eighty-two million of dollars." We have no later returns from which we can correctly ascertain the amount loaned by the banks to the speculators, so we must content ourselves with these. But we have no reason to suppose that the banks have been less indulgent to the speculators since this report was made.

The loaning of bank funds to speculators is not an evil of recent date.

Perhaps the most noted example of reckless loaning in this country was by the SECOND UNITED STATES BANK chartered by Congress in 1816. Its capital was $35,000,000. The operations of the bank having become very corrupt, in 1841 a committee was appointed by Congress to examine into its affairs. And what did they find? On the 21st of December, 1840, loans were made to several incorporated companies amounting to $1,211,163, including one of $502,222 to the Wilmington Railroad. Discounts to the amount of $740,056 had been made with at least six months to run; and the balance was loaned payable in one year. Nine companies had discounts of over $100,000 each. A great deal of suspended indebtedness was discovered. Fifty-two individual firms and companies were severally charged with more than $20,000; twenty-nine had debts exceeding $50.000 each, and nine having each a debt of $100,000. Six concerns were charged with $2,314,000. One firm in Philadelphia, between August, 1835, and November, 1837. received accommodation to the extent of $4,213,878, more than half of which was obtained in the year 1837. Mr. SAMUEL JAUDON, when he resigned as cashier of the bank, upon being appointed as its foreign agent, was a debtor to the extent of $408,389, and the ingenious reason given by the directors for giving him an enormous salary as cashier, was on account of his heavy indebtedness to the bank. A former cashier was charged with $104,000. At the same time, the first assistant cashier was indebted to the bank in the sum of $115,000, which was finally increased to $326,382. He then graduated as assistant and was made cashier of the institution. If any one would like to know what the two last-named officers did with their funds, it may be answered that they invested them in the Camden and Woodbury, Wilmington, and Grand Gulf Railroads, and in the Dauphin and Lycoming coal lands. When the stocks of these various companies were given up as worthless, they were transferred to the bank in satisfaction of the indebtedness of their holders. In 1836 the amount loaned upon the pledge of "fancy stocks" was nearly $20,400,000. The same year an advance was made to A. G. JAUDON to enable him to purchase cotton which was remitted to BARING, BROTHERS & Co., of Liverpool. "The derangement of the currency," said Mr. BIDDLE, when explaining the effect of this purchase to Mr.

ADAMS, "placed the staples of the South entirely at the mercy of the foreign purchaser, who could have dictated the terms of sale to the prostrated planter. It was thought proper to avert the evil by employing a large portion of the capital of the bank in making advances on southern produce."

Why have banks assisted speculators so much? First.—As deposits are generally made payable on call, banks have believed it to be a wise policy to loan large portions in this manner; for, if they are asked to pay heavy sums, they can easily be obtained. If loans were made to brokers with stocks and gold as collateral, the loans were safe, and they could be repaid at a moment's notice. The banks never dreamed that if a great many wanted to realize quickly, no one could: and, consequently, that such loans were not more likely to be paid than others.

Secondly.—By making call loans, a greater portion of deposits can be loaned. The banks do not dare to loan all their funds upon time, because these institutions are liable to heavy demands at any moment. In making call loans, however, they can discount more heavily as they can call in such loans whenever they desire. By this policy dividends are increased.

Thirdly.—Speculators have offered higher rates for money. It is humiliating to us as a nation, that speculators have for years been able to outbid legitimate and healthy business for money. Yet, having offered rates of interest which merchants could not afford to pay, speculators have been accommodated and merchants left without help.

Fourthly.—Another reason impelling banks to make call loans was that, as they had encouraged deposits by offering interest at three to five per cent. on them, it became necessary to loan these deposits to avoid loss. The only chance to make anything was to loan immediately and at higher rates than those paid to depositors. They had, it is true, the precedent of banks abroad for offering interest on deposits, though few of them offer so much as do our own. The banks have thus diverted a large portion of their resources to speculative purposes.* Not all the banks have been guilty of this. The offenders are principally in New York City, and even there many honorable exceptions may be found.

We have given some of the reasons for condemning speculation. We have seen that banks greatly assist speculators by loaning them funds to carry on their operations. The question arises, how can banks be prevented from rendering this assistance?

Prohibit, by law, the payment of interest on deposits. The custom of paying interest on deposits has found many defenders and opponents. It unquestionably tends to increase deposits, but the evils arising from the improper use of them, if interest be paid, far outweighs the benefits of resorting to this method of encouraging an increase. This remark has no application to the payment of interest upon special deposits—that is, those made for a specified time, but only to those made daily and in the usual course of business. To pay interest on these—especially to pay high rates—we believe to be contrary to sound banking. After the terrible crisis of 1857, the Clearing-House Association of the New York City banks appointed a committee to investigate into this subject. At that time all except six out of forty-six banks composing the association united in an agreement not to pay interest on deposits. This fact was stated by the committee in their report. The subject was considered by them with marked

---

* It is a thing of common occurrence for merchants, manufacturers, and others who denounce the action of banks in loaning to speculators, to loan their own deposits to such banks, in order to get interest upon them. Thus their greed for gain leads men to feed the speculators whom they denounce.

ability, and the conclusions at which they arrived were summed up near the close of their report. The practice of paying interest upon deposits they declared was, —

1. Inherently unsound.
2. That it tends to weaken the legitimate commerce of the country, and to disturb the regularity of the business of the city.
3. That no bank can safely and profitably practice it.
4. That it tends to interfere with the efficiency and stability of our banks, and with the harmony of their intercourse with each other.
5. That its discontinuance will not divert any substantial deposits from this city.
6. That the reasons for its discontinuance are daily increasing.
7. That it has, under like conditions, no fair precedent in older countries.
8. That, as it exists here, it has been unjustly applied.

After sixteen years more of experience in banking, the same Clearing-House Association appointed another committee to consider "What reforms are required in the operations of banks with each other and the public to increase the security of their business; and, first and most prominent, they recommend that the banks entirely discontinue the payment of interest upon deposits, whether directly or indirectly."

With this accumulated experience before us, the National Government ought not to hesitate in enacting a law forbidding the payment of interest upon deposits. The fact that a different custom prevails abroad is of no force here, because our monetary system is so unlike any other. Besides, the BANK OF ENGLAND, the largest in the world, has never paid interest on deposits. Let such a law be passed and banking will become a sounder business, while the country at large will be greatly benefited by the severe checks which speculation must receive.*

It will be said, why interfere with the action of the banks? Why not permit them to act according to their own judgment? The common saying among bankers is: "Take care of the currency; make that as secure as possible, but do not interfere with the *business* of the banks." What is implied in this saying? It is that banks have the right to manage their own affairs, and that if allowed to exercise it, banking would become a more profitable business. This is the reason why they so loudly clamor for non-interference in their concerns.† Profits are reduced thereby. Moreover, many bankers are very outspoken in their claim that it is beyond the scope of the government to undertake the supervision and direction of banks. To this claim they add this additional consideration that whenever the government has undertaken the supervision and control of them, no benefit has resulted therefrom, either to the banks or to the public.

Banks are corporations created by the government, not for the good of the corporators alone, but also for the good of the public. Corporations, in general, seem to be quite innocent of this truth now-a-days. They have grown to think that corporations are wholly one-sided affairs, created only for the benefit of themselves, and therefore that the government has no right to put any

---

* It is evident that if the banks are forbidden to pay interest on deposits, of course, the country banks will thereafter retain all of their own deposits. It is true that it would be necessary to keep small deposits with the city banks in order to have the drafts upon the city banks paid upon presentment. But all the deposits of country banks, beyond the quantity required for this purpose, would be retained. Hence the city banks would be deprived of these numerous and perennial fountains from whence speculators have been fed. In 1870, the amount thus furnished by the country to the city banks amounted to $72,272,790.36. The speculators, therefore, would be so weakened from this loss of blood that they could not carry on their operations with the same degree of energy as before.

† See article in *Banker's Magazine*—Banking Amendments—July, 1870.

checks in the way of their earning the greatest gains. The time has fully come when corporations must unlearn this error, and remember that they are endowed with corporate life, not for their good merely, but for that of the public. It is very absurd to suppose that the government creates an institution to prey upon the public, and from which it is to derive no benefit. If the government, by mistake or otherwise, has endowed such an institution with a legal existence, it should be removed as speedily as possible. A corporation which is not beneficial to the public as well as to the corporators, has no place in a well-organized society. Is it not true that corporations gain more from the public than the public from them? Indeed, would one ever be created if this were not the case? And if such be the case, may it not be doubted whether the government should ever create a corporation? Surely, if such institutions are authorized, the government ought to watch over them with a jealous care, lest the public suffer too much, rather than the corporators lose too much, therefrom. The banks must remember that they are corporations, and consequently that the government has a right to interfere, and that it is the duty of the government to interfere, whenever they are not conducting their business in harmony with the best interests of society. Nothing can be plainer than this. If banks are making imprudent or unwise loans, if they are abusing in any way the laws of their corporate life, it is the duty of the government to correct such abuses by applying the most efficacious remedies.

We have seen that banks loan a large portion of their funds to speculators; that banks injure the mercantile community, which includes the productive class of the country, by withdrawing the money it needs; and that this evil can be corrected, in part at least, by forbidding the banks from paying interest on deposits. What is clearer than that the government should lay this restriction upon them?

The banks say, "Oh! you do this, and we cannot live. It is just what our enemies, the private bankers, wish to have done, in order to crush us out." Very well. If you cannot live without injuring the public more than you benefit it, you ought to be crushed out. Besides, you are not obliged to exist at all. If you cannot make money enough without making call loans, and by paying interest on deposits in order to get the money to make them, then retire from corporate banking, and seek some other occupation. The public can be deprived of the benefits you confer upon it with less loss to itself than if you are permitted to live, and they be chased by a pack of greedy speculators. If you cannot feed the good fish without feeding the sharks, it is certainly preferable that each should pick up a living in other ways. For the producer knows that when both are left to procure their own subsistence, he will succeed whether the speculator does or not. The government may wisely go further than this in forbidding the payment of interest on deposits. It may forbid the banks from taking gold as collateral for loans. No one will keep gold except for speculative purposes, and the fact that one wishes to use it as a basis for loans is evidence enough that he holds it merely for speculation. The banks know this. Nothing is plainer than that if such a law were passed it would diminish speculation in gold by cutting off the supply of funds to pay for the gold purchased.

XIII.

THE INFLUENCE OF CREDIT ON PRICES.

A great deal has been written concerning the influence of credit on prices. Yet the subject is simple enough. Suppose the banks increase their circulation to one thousand millions of dollars, promising to redeem it on demand in gold? Would this enormous amount of promises have any influence on prices? Probably. Supposing the people had confidence that they would be surely paid according to their tenor, they would have precisely the same influence on prices as a like increase of gold. If the addition of so much gold would increase prices, so would these bank notes which are substituted for it. So long as people have full confidence that gold and bank notes, or other instruments of credit, are really and instantly convertible into each other, the influence of each upon prices is the same.* Thus far there is no difficulty with the nature of credit.

At this point we must distinguish between a depreciation in the measure of value and an increase of prices. In the strict sense of the phrase, as we have seen, no such distinction can be made,

---

* "There is scarcely any shape into which credit can be cast, in which it will not at times be called to perform the functions of money, and whether that shape be a bank note or a bill of exchange, or a banker's check, the process is in every essential particular the same, and the result is the same." FULLARTON on the *Reg. of Currencies*, p. 29.

but popularly there is one. We are all familiar with the fact that the prices of things were greatly enhanced during the late war, measured or estimated in paper dollars—that is, legal-tender notes, which were given in exchange. Yet prices remained nearly the same, measured by the gold standard, for as large a quantity of wheat could be purchased for the same amount of gold as before. What, therefore, happened was not, popularly speaking, an increase of prices (suppposing the price of things measured in gold to remain the same), but a depreciation in the measure of value. The paper measure was not equivalent to the metallic measure.

The fall and rise of prices is governed directly or immediately by the law of supply or demand, though a very vague and defective law. Then demand, in turn, is sharpened by the amount of money which the buyer may have to purchase with. If he have plenty, then he will purchase more; if short, he will purchase less. But if he have credit, this is a substitute for money; and if it be equivalent to money, then he buys just as cheaply as though money was paid. "Credit, in short," says Mr. MILL,* "has exactly the same purchasing power with money, and as money tells upon prices, not simply in proportion to its amount, but to its amount multiplied by the number of times it changes hands, so also does credit, and credit transferable from hand to hand is in that proportion more potent than credit which only performs one purchase."

Confidence is rarely perfect. The merchant knows that custom-

* *Princ of Pol. Econ.*, vol. 2, p. 75, (Fifth Lond ed.) There is no contradiction in MILL's writings about credit, as MACLEOD has earnestly labored to show. *Prin. of Econ. Philos*, pp. 616-673, (2d ed.) When MILL says that credit is not capital, he means by credit the power to borrow money. The transfer of money is not the creation, but merely the transfer of capital The power to buy goods, etc., without giving anything in exchange, this is capital, and MILL does not deny it. He is silent in respect to it

ers are frequently failing in business. He expects that among all to whom he sells, some will fail to pay. Hence in fixing a price at which he shall sell his goods, an additional price is charged to cover this prospective loss. In other words, he becomes his own insurer against loss arising from the failure of customers. The cost of this insurance is an additional price to the goods which, of course, would not be charged if immediate payment were made.

It is true, therefore, that price depends immediately upon supply and demand which, in turn, is very much increased by the giving of credit. Says FAWCETT: "If it were not for credit, the demand for commodities would frequently be much less than it is. In fact, when credit is freely given, the demand for a commodity may increase without any assignable limits."*

How are sellers able to give so much credit? By obtaining it from those of whom they buy, and from others, though principally from banks. The latter furnish credit by exchanging notes with their customers. The reason why the customer seeks to exchange is because bank notes inspire a higher confidence than his own. The bank may be willing to trust him, but others are not; or, it may be more advantageous to owe the bank than the party to whom the notes of the bank are paid.

Let us now begin at the other end of the chain of influences acting on price. If the banks, or the individuals, did not in the first place loan their credit, others could not buy so many goods,

* *Man. of Polit. Econ.*, p. 387, (3d ed.) Says Prof. PRICE: "What raises prices universally is buying, whether that buying be made by the transfer of an article of equivalent value, such as coin, or whether the goods are sold and delivered without payment being made at the time. The greater the buying, either on trust or with coin, the stronger will be the tendency of the articles in demand to rise in price. The particular manner in which evidence is obtained of goods having been delivered without payment, and security taken, by bill or note, that this deferred payment shall in due time be effected, is utterly insignificant, so far as concerns any action on prices."—*Princ. of Currency*, p. 168.

hence, there would not be so great demand for them, and consequently, their price would be less. Credit from whomsoever derived, increases price by stimulating and feeding demand. Therefore, the banks are not alone justly chargeable with the evils springing out of the credit system, according to the opinion of some writers, but only in common with all who give credit, and in proportion to the respective amounts given by banks and individuals.

XIV.

ON LEGAL INTERFERENCE WITH THE LOAN OF MONEY, PAYMENT OF LABOR, AND CONTRACTS OF CORPORATIONS.

In this chapter we shall consider the right and expediency of the State to interfere in the making of three classes of contracts, namely: Contracts for Labor, Usury Laws, and Contracts of Corporations, leaving the question of enacting protective laws to be discussed in the chapter following.

Why does any one seek State interference in these matters? A true answer reveals the selfishness and tyranny of mankind.

Employers generally have wealth, either inherited or acquired, while the laborer's wealth is in brain and limb. Let his body die or be impaired by accident or disease, and his wealth is diminished or forever lost.

From the situation of the parties, it is evident that the employer has the advantage. Of course, his wealth will not increase without the co-operation of labor; but if he cannot employ it upon his own terms, he can wait till the laborer yields. Not so fortunate is the son of toil. He must take what he can get or starve. Work or starvation is the only alternative of his life. The capitalist, knowing this, profits by the fact in offering terms of wages. He really fixes the price of labor himself; the other party merely assents to the sum offered. This is the true situation of the parties when it is fully unmasked. The law of demand and supply has many holes in it, and here is a big one. The laws governing human action cannot be half as clearly traced as the laws of nature and of God. The law of demand and supply, which is thought to have such a universal operation in the field of economic science, is only a crooked brook that not infrequently is absorbed in the sands of selfishness, or diverted by superior force. In the older countries, especially, the capitalist has a tremendous advantage, because the quantity of labor is practically unlimited. There not being work enough for all, the employer dictates his own terms; even if all had work, the mind of the employer might not change. Wealth would still hold the key to the situation.

Thus we come in sight of the first question touching contracts for labor—has the State a right to interfere in behalf of the laborer in fixing the terms of the contract for his services; and if the right be admitted, is it expedient for the State to exercise this right? Let us follow the case of the laborer one step farther. It is not for the interest of the capitalist to suffer labor to perish; if he did, his own profits would be lost. He seeks to retain him, paying the smallest sum necessary for that purpose.

The beautiful rule of equity would divide profits differently. It would give the employed a reasonable sum for his work, and the capitalist a like sum for the use of his capital and skill, and divide the balance, if any remained, fairly between the two. This is not the way, however, that the capitalist generally looks at the question. He seeks to find out the least for which he can employ laborers and keep them from starving, and retains the rest of the income flowing from his business for himself.

This, of course, is stating the question in the broadest way, and several objections may be made to this form of statement. In the first place, some capitalists divide their profits equitably with their workmen. Splendid instances of this have occurred in the history of British industry. Various trials are making in all the more enlightened countries to devise a practicable mode of dividing profits between employer and employed. In the second place, the laborer in this country exercises greater freedom in making contracts than in the old. This happens from the smaller number of workmen in proportion to the amount of work to be done, and from the abundance of unoccupied land which he can improve if he fails to make a satisfactory agreement with his employer.

This, then, is the second question raised by the laborer—shall not the Government make laws fairly distributing the profits between the two classes? The argument upon which he founds his claim is briefly this, that he has contributed the larger share in earning the profits, hence they ought fairly to be divided.

A similar foundation of facts lies beneath the usury law. "The lender" so the borrower declares, "means to oppress me; he has the same advantage over me that the employer has over the laborer." The lender, for example, exacts ten per cent. for the use of his money, and will not loan it for less. Having ample means to supply his wants, even if a part of his property is not earning interest, he can suffer a portion of it to lie idle for the purpose of bringing the borrower to terms. He watches the borrower, pries into his business, and finds out how much he is making, and then guesses how high a rate of interest he will pay for the use of the money. The more profitable the business, the more he will pay rather than go without it. The lender marks up to the highest notch, and believes that by waiting, the borrower will crawl up to his figures.

The borrower says: "This advantage you ought not to take," and he calls upon the State to prevent the lender from reaping it. He seeks to get upon an even plane with the lender by force of law. Like the capitalist in fixing the rate of wages, the money lender would fix the rate of interest so high as to reserve the smallest amount of profits to the borrower accruing from the money loaned. If the borrower be a merchant, the lender says to himself: "How much money is A making in his business," and according to the conclusion is the rate of interest asked.

If a usury law is passed to prevent the lender from obtaining too great a reward, the same principle may be applied to prevent the farmer from charging too much for his potatoes. As a fact, however, there is not much danger of lenders generally charging excessively high rates of interest. This is especially true of banks. They keep within bounds. During the panic of 1873, when money commanded enormous prices, banks supplied their customers, so far as they supplied them at all, at the old rates. Individuals are disposed to charge higher rates than banking institutions. The reason is, banks are loaning the money of other people, and are more merciful than individuals when lending their own. This is especially true of savings banks. They consider what a man can afford to pay. But if a usury law is passed to prevent banks from taking advantages, logically it should cover all cases. All men who are taking advantage of others by selling at too profitable rates, must have the law applied to them.

From this rapid survey of the motives leading men to seek the interference of Government, it will be seen that the reason is to help one class in. or to prevent one class from, getting an advantage over another. It is to enable one or more persons in obtaining an advantage over the rest, or in neutralizing an advantage already possessed.

Even Government itself, in our opinion, owes its origin to this very desire of one man, or a set of men, to obtain an advantage over others. In the beginning, one or a few ruled the rest by virtue of superior force or wisdom, as they rule now. If it were not to obtain an advantage in accumulating property, it was to gratify the desire for governing, to have ideas and opinions triumph. We do not believe that Government was founded in acquiescence or agreement; a pure democracy is the consummate flower of civilization. The lesson taught by history is that the one-man power existed in the beginning; the right of the people to rule and choose their own sovereigns is a principle issuing from a long and bitter warfare. This usurpation, in the first instance, was to get some sort of an advantage by an individual or by a few, and to retain it if possible. It is only another illustration of the spirit prevailing in all times and countries of getting advantages whenever it is possible; of the strong ruling the weak. A democratic Government is no exception. The nearer the approach to a pure democracy, the more equal is the liberty and the power enjoyed; but in the fairest Government that has yet bloomed on the face of the earth, a few have led public opinion and ruled the rest, and the mass have been willing to follow. They have realized, to some extent, their own weakness, and the need of rulers. No king, unaided and alone, has made and executed law for the rest. But kings have identified the interests of a class with their own, and so have been able to tyrannize over the greater number. The wider the ruling class, the more distributed is the advantage, yet, even in our own beloved land, who will deny that the dominant party has always used the machinery of Government for personal ends, and will thus use it till parties are less deeply immersed in selfishness than they are now? This is the principal source of a party's strength, that it can use the Government for the advantage of its members. Let party service become purely disinterested, and the zeal of most of its members would cool off as suddenly and as greatly as their bodies would if placed around the north pole in the dead of winter.

From this analysis of the motives of people in making agreements, we have seen that the assistance of the State is sought to balance the situation of those opposed to each other in business so that they may be able to contract on fair terms; or else to make the advantages already possessed by any one greater still. It is either to even up the condition of mankind, or to make those well-off better-off.

Having stated the problem in the broadest manner, we shall proceed to consider whether the Government has a right to interfere in the cases mentioned. This involves a consideration of the functions of Government. By no shorter cut can we reach any satisfactory conclusion.

One class of very able thinkers maintain that every man is entitled to the fullest liberty subject to the enjoyment of like liberty by every other individual. Not till a person breaks in upon the liberty of another, has the Government a right to interfere. This class sometimes state their doctrine in a shorter way, namely, that the cardinal duty of the State is to administer justice. Whether right or wrong, they are entitled to the merit of stating the functions of Government more precisely than any other class. They have carved out its functions exactly and logically in many minute particulars. But if those holding a different view are less able to state the exact functions of Government in some respects, the reason is, that ascribing broader functions to Government, it is more difficult, nay impossible, to draw any hard and fast line defining those functions.* Yet, may not this very impossibility to realize or express the broader functions of Government, indicate that the view is deeper and nearer the truth? The truths most clearly seen are those lying nearest to us and which are the most shallow; beneath the crust we grope in darkness and difficulty, yet we know that the solid earth is there, although we can tell less about its qualities. There is a way of getting a clear notion of a thing, as COMTE got of philosophy, by throwing out all difficult questions and maintaining that they do not exist; but all minds will not be satisfied with solving questions in this way. According to our way of thinking, those who have obtained such limpid and simple views of Government have dealt with the question very much as COMTE treated philosophy.

It may be noted that those holding the narrow view of Government—which is the one first stated—support it by reference to the origin of Government itself. Such a reference is wholly useless, unless it be maintained that society is bound by the original conception of a Government. If society is left free to change its Government, either in enlarging or narrowing its functions, its original structure is not of the slightest consequence.

No society can impose terms upon their successors. The past has no claim upon the future and cannot dictate to it. We may accept what others have bequeathed, but there is no law compel-

* Says Mr. MILL: "In attempting to enumerate the necessary functions of Government, we find them to be considerably more multifarious than most people are at first aware of, and not capable of being circumscribed by those very definite lines of demarcation, which, in the inconsiderateness of popular discussion, it is often attempted to draw around them."—*Princ. of Polit. Econ.*, vol. 2, p. 387.

ing a legatee to accept a legacy. Society is progressive and needs a progressive form of Government. That society is of this character, SPENCER and the rest of his class holding to the narrow functions of Government, will not deny; indeed, it figures more prominently in their doctrine of Government than in ours. But if mankind are growing better, they need a better Government to suit their improving condition. To maintain that the same kind of Government is best, both for the rudest and most enlightened, is ridiculous. In Christian theology it has come to be a recognized truth, that as intelligence increases, and things spiritual are more clearly discerned, theology changes and improves. Instead of being a perfected system, the profounder study of the Scriptures with the new light reflected upon them by modern scholarship, theology is brought nearer to perfection. The analogy holds in respect to Government, as mankind increase in intelligence and goodness, and become more inter-related, their conceptions of Government change to suit their advanced condition.

If this be granted, we care not whether the original Government was founded upon the principle enunciated by HERBERT SPENCER, or upon some other, or upon no principle at all; the sole question is, what is the best Government for mankind to-day? It is possible that SPENCER's principle—mankind should be allowed to exercise the fullest liberty subject to the exercise of like liberty by every other individual—is the correct one. In enunciating it, though, SPENCER undoubtedly thought it was in harmony with a principle lying still deeper, namely, that such a limitation of the functions of Government was best for the good of the individual. Certainly he would not deny that this was the end he had in view both in prescribing a Government and in finding its limitations; hence, in determining the functions of Government, we must inquire, what kind of one is best for us? How shall its powers be limited so as not to interfere with our highest progress? Here is the true starting point whence all inquirers set out.

Nor will it be much questioned that the highest good of each individual is in harmony with the highest good of every other, thus making no difference, when looking after the best Government, whether we fix our eyes upon the good of one or the good of all. We need spend no time, then, over this point.

A Government having for its end the highest good of its subjects cannot be stationary in its scope, it must change. For, as our ideas of good approach nearer to the absolute and perfect truth, Government must change to correspond with them. Suppose the only good thought of in the beginning was material and low, Government evidently must correspond with it; as the conception of good grows and blossoms fair and beautiful, a corresponding change is wrought in the nature and province of Government. The symbol of man himself, and yet an instrument to make him better, it must ever change to promote his good. No conception of a definite Government for all time is possible by reason of the incessant changes of human life; nor is a fixed Government to be desired.

As a general rule, Government promotes the good of those farthest advanced least; this is easily enough seen. All laws are a succession of compromises between the wants of the better class and other classes not so good. Laws really represent the complete wishes of no class, being more severe perhaps than one class desires, and not severe enough for another. This is especially true of penal laws, nevertheless all are more beneficent in their operation upon one class than upon another. Laws operating to the equal advantage of every member of society are scarce. Still, if a law does not always reflect the most advanced sentiment of society it is an approximation to it, and by and by becomes the sentiment of many, affording some degree of protection. So the doctrine that law has an educating and uplifting power, if actually containing more truth than some believe, is not wholly false; although the danger of the non-enforcement of such laws, even if enacted, is too great to warrant their enactment upon this ground. The evil growing out of a law which cannot be enforced, because opposed to the sentiment and force necessary to execute it, is greater than its educating power. The law is for the law-breaker, not the keeper of it; hence it must be a law that can be enforced. Law for those who are always willing to keep them are not laws, only rules.

As the civilization of society increases, each member is more closely inter-related to every other member, affects him more, and so the functions of Government must widen. Prof. Huxley has stated this truth in an admirable way. "The higher the state of civilization, the more completely do the actions of one member of the social body influence all the rest, and the less possible is it for any one man to do a wrong thing without interfering, more or less, with the freedom of all his fellow-citizens." Consequently, if the functions of Government were pared down to self-protection merely, yet as the actions of men affect each other more and more, the sphere of Government must continually widen in order to furnish that self-protection which even Spencer admits Government is bound to furnish.

Spencer and those holding similar views of Government advocate the largest measure of liberty for all, because they believe that human improvement is most rapid under that condition. They will not deny that man should aim to reach the highest end known to himself, and that Government, so far as possible, ought to be used to bear him upward toward that end. In fact, they cannot deny these statements without involving themselves in contradiction. For, the very reason why they have set up the liberty-theory is because man will develop most rapidly under it. Perhaps it is not correct to say that Government is a reformatory or remedial institution, yet it is, and there is no disputing the fact. The end of all wholesome laws is to improve society by punishing crime and restraining wrong-doing. All punishment is aimed at both things—to render justice and prevent the commission of crime. Is it true that man will flourish best in the exercise of the highest liberty? This is the belief of those who narrow down the functions of Government. Are plants the most beautiful in a state of nature? Are they not made fairer by cultivation? Do not careful watching, pruning, and watering of them, increase their beauty of form and color? Who questions that men improve more rapidly under a state of cultivation? What progress would the student make in his earlier years if left to the exercise of the largest liberty in the choice of his studies and in the mode of pursuing them? Who ever heard of a savage blossoming in beauty unto perfection like the most perfect flower? The finest intellect, art, morality, religion, is the product of the greatest care, toil, and restraint in living. The State can do something in the way of instructing and directing men; how much it can do is a question. Undoubtedly it cannot do half as much as the popular mind believes it can. The opinions of many are altogether too sanguine concerning the educating and restraining power of the State. The State has often undertaken to do things which it ought to have left alone. It is not true, however, that the State contains no civilizing power, or that men will develop most rapidly when left to themselves, or with other helps than the State, which they may call into use. A great many do not want to help themselves and would not improve their condition if they could. Firmly as we believe in the ultimate perfectibility of man, he is now fearfully depraved and his aspirations to improve are so feeble as to be easily overpowered by his evil genius of a will. SPENCER does not consider sufficiently the evil tendencies of man and the need of his coercion and severe discipline. He is all the better for every proper restraint and check. He is like a garden vegetable that will spend all its force in extending its vines or branches, and bearing no fruit, unless it be clipped in its luxuriant growth. We admit that a great many State checks have dwarfed rather than developed the powers of man, but not always. SPENCER has illustrated the first fact in a most brilliant manner, and by so doing has popularized a theory which we believe to be unsound and pernicious to society. Government has done its good things as well as its evil ones, and the former ought not be forgotten in the condemnation of the latter. SPENCER has proved beyond a question that the Government is continually attempting to do what it cannot do, or can only do in a most feeble way. It were much better for both Government and people that it had never undertaken many things it has. This is the strongest side of SPENCER's teachings, the showing up of the numerous failures of Government to essay the impossible and the impracticable.

We have previously observed that all people are living for the highest good. This is true in a general sense. It is of no consequence in what phraseology this idea is clothed, whether it be simply the highest, or the highest end, or the highest good, or the greatest happiness, or in some other clothing. The sole conception is that every person has some supreme purpose in life, although that purpose may be as different with individuals as they are unlike in character. The highest end of one may be in serving GOD, that of another in getting drunk; but that each has a supreme end in view will not be denied.

Now, we maintain that the end of Government ought to be what it practically is in many cases, to assist society in attaining its highest end. Everything Government can do in that direction is within its province; by this end are its powers limited.

This object of Government has the merit of simplicity and comprehensiveness. It is sanctioned by experience and by great names, though perhaps no one has expressed the idea in a nobler and briefer way than LOCKE, who declared, "That the end of Government is the good of mankind."

If this view be correct, the functions of Government will change with the growing conceptions of the highest end of living. There can be no permanent sphere for it, because of the incessant changes going on in society. If mankind made no progress and suffered no decline, then it would be easy enough to mark out the track for Government to pursue, and give it permanent bounds. But we are progressing. Through blood and tears man is looking up and struggling to reach a better state. The weeds of misery grow more luxuriantly than the good and hide its fairest flowers; nevertheless the good also grows and one day will bloom in perfect beauty. No impartial reader of history can fail to see that the world is overcoming evil and attaining to higher notions of the true end of life. With this advancement, a strange and direful confusion would be wrought were Government to continue in a narrow, worn-out track.

It does not follow, in the spreading of Government over a broader field, that legal penalties will increase in number and heaviness. Quite the contrary. They will be fewer and lighter with better living. Only murder is punished with death in this country and GREAT BRITAIN, yet in COLERIDGE'S time the forging of a frank upon a letter was punished in this manner. Laws increase in number with the progress of civilization, but they approximate more and more toward rules for the conduct of the individual.

We imagine that in a perfect moral Government, there will be only rules governing the intercourse of its members, without any penalties whatever, for they would be unnecessary; but rules will not be less numerous because there are none to break them. Rules are needed for our guidance even if there be no disposition to set them aside.

In the establishment and maintenance of Government for this object, the good of man, the believer in its divine origin and the scouter of this doctrine can agree. For the conception of the part which Government should play in reaching the highest, is the conception of a majority or of a smaller number of those living under it. We have adverted to the manner in which Government, in our opinion, sprang into being. Practically, every Government is that of the few, one man by virtue of greater force, or surpassing ability, or rascality, may govern, but after all, more than one alone must govern any people. He must have friends to support him, else his Government will inevitably be overturned. Even the most despotic Government has several rulers. Control obtained of the army by Napoleon, who united their interests with his own, enabled him to plant himself on the throne of France. Be a Government ever so democratic a few leaders rule. There may be more of them at one time than at another, nevertheless a few do the thinking and controlling for society. Only now and then is one found who thinks; fewer act. Those who both think and act have always controlled society, and they always will. The functions of Government are not always those which B and C would set up, but are those set up by the leaders of society. If the greatest liberty be allowed, this is thought to be conducive to the best interests of all; if the least liberty is tolerated, the reason is the same. Hence the functions of Government may be few or many; the end of it may be very low or very exalted. It may permit the vilest practices, or it may prevent all such. In either case, the believer in a divine order would see that so far as Government went, it was an approximation to the Government of God, which is one day to prevail (according to his belief), while another class would only see that the idea of God or a divine order was absurd. The former class might mourn over the rules of society because they contained such faint glimmerings of the highest end of man and of the best Government for him, yet he would acknowledge that the rulers saw a real glimmer of these things, however faint.

Let us not leave this point quite yet. The believer in the Divine affirms that a time is coming when all will be perfect, obeying a perfect moral law, which God will give. The seer looks upon the present Government as a shadow and an indication of the perfect one to come. So far as Government goes, it is a revelation of God to its makers and upholders, the unfolding of the Divine idea, either consciously or unconsciously to themselves. The seer beholds in the progress of mankind and in the progress of Government a glimpse of the perfect day. Crude is the Divine idea within, but it is there, and will not die for it is planted and nurtured by God.

The disbeliever in the supernatural says: "This is all nonsense."

He affirms that Government is a purely human contrivance. "Very well," replies the other, "we can live together, for we agree that both are living for the highest, and that the object of Government is to help us on in our way. We agree as to whither Government is tending, and what its functions shall be; we only differ as to the source whence the laws proceed." The one claims they are pure human expedients; the other, the expression, though imperfect, of the Divine will.

Thus it is seen that as all live for the same absolute end, though not for the same relative one, the functions of Government maintained by both classes are the same, and are determined by the collective mind controlling society. Hence, Government is agreeable to all. Who is right as to the human or Divine power entering into Government and making it what it is, the future alone can reveal. If the Christian's belief is right, he will expect to see Government growing more and more into the likeness of the eternal Government of GOD, till the human contrivance is absorbed and lost in the splendor of the other. If he is wrong, then he must confess that Government is purely a human device.

Having shown what, in our opinion, is the true end of Government, it remains for us to answer the questions announced in the beginning. Whether Government shall interfere in any of the cases mentioned, depends upon the effect of such interference upon society. We have shown that the reason why Government interference is sought in any case is to get, or to prevent, an advantage of one person or more over others. In our opinion, Government ought to assist no class in obtaining an advantage over another, whether the class be living in the same country or elsewhere. Government must preserve equality, and not make inequalities greater. This is clear enough. But how far it shall go in the way of leveling the inequalities now existing; how far in the way of preventing advantages from being taken, is a question of expediency. We do not question the right of the Government to go very far in this direction. We do not believe that Government is to exist in a land of darkness and in the shadow of death, to see one class crush down another by monopoly and oppression, and put forth no power to save the wronged and the weak. Such destruction of the interests of a class is the funeral of the nation in more senses than one. And the nation has a right, if it thinks best, to stop these things. This, of course, is predicated upon the idea that it has the ability to prevent undue advantages if it pleases. If it cannot, that is the end of the matter.

Government has certainly gone the whole length for which we contend. What is the object of a usury law save to prevent one class from taking advantage of another? The money lender oppresses the borrower in exacting excessively high rates of interest. The law is aimed to prevent this. But the principle involved in the law by which Government interferes to prevent the taking of an undue advantage in the loan of money, applies with equal force to every thing else which men buy, sell, and use.

Some claim that Government has the right to step in and regulate the charge for the use of money because it is the creation of Government; but this claim is thinner than gossamer. Government is not the creator of value. That depends upon the desire for a thing and the difficulty of attaining it. Value is purely within human control. Is not the five-dollar gold-piece worth just as much in an uncoined as in a coined state? Its value is dependent upon its weight and purity, and not upon the work of the Government. Remove every trace of the Governmental superscription, re-melt a gold coin, and the shapeless piece of yellow metal will be worth as much as before. This proves that Government exercises no peculiar power or charm over money; hence, it has no right by virtue of anything it does to money to say how much shall be paid for the use thereof. There is no mysterious property clinging to money. The sole difference between money and other things is that the former, generally, has a wider purchasing power. We have tried to prove that Government has a right of determining how much shall be paid for the use of money, but solely upon the ground of preventing one citizen from taking an unjust advantage of another.

Whether Government should exercise this right depends upon two questions: first, whether the advantage be so great as to call for Government interference; secondly, whether it has the power to interfere effectively. Whatever the past may show, we believe that the oppression now is not great enough to warrant interference on the part of the State; and if we admitted that it was, it is clear as crystal that Government cannot interfere effectively to prevent advantages from being taken. This has been proved over and over again. There is not a usury law in existence, in any State of the Union, to-day, that is anything but a dead letter, buried out of sight and almost out of memory. So much for a usury law.

The two questions concerning the payment of labor may be answered together. Government has a perfect right to interfere, upon the grounds assumed in enacting a usury law, to prevent the taking of an improper advantage. Whenever the advantages between capitalist and laborers become too great on the one side or on the other, Government may interfere to prevent their occurrence. If the capitalist squeezes the laborer too hard, or divides too small a portion of the profits, or the laborer demands too much pay, Government has the right, according to the foregoing reasoning, of determining what the one shall pay and the other receive. As for the need, or practicability of any such interference on the part of the State, there is none. Both adjust their differences more easily than the State could for them; indeed, it would cut a sorry figure if attempting to make an adjustment.

We come now to the last class of contracts, those of corporations. These are creatures of the State, they have their birth and existence by the favor of the State, yet the longer they live, the more do they forget their parentage and dependence. They seem to think, after a time, that they are very much like other folks, entitled to all the rights they have and many besides. The people must not forget the true origin and character of corporations. With their gigantic growth in this country, with their enormous aggregation of wealth, they deserve the most careful watching. For the most superficial glance at their working and aims shows that they propose to ask a great deal more of the State in the future, and to abuse the mother which gave them being. Their creation was justified on the ground that they would prove beneficial to the community, but we fear of their becoming its curse.

It must not be forgotten that corporations are creatures of the State and subject to its control. There is no analogy between them and individuals. We have shown how the State should govern its members, for the good of all. Corporations must be governed in the same manner. So long as they are conducted for the best interest of all, they should be let alone. When conducted otherwise, the State must not hesitate to interfere and prescribe such checks as are called for by the good of society, and see that they are enforced. The State must not be beguiled by the claims and arrogance of her own children, who are growing bolder as they increase in wealth and power. For there is danger, unless the State be watchful and keeps them in proper restraint, that they will become more powerful than the State itself.

XV.

THE ADVANTAGES OF EXCHANGE.

Many still hug the delusion that in every exchange one party or the other must be the loser. They cannot believe that exchanges may be beneficial to all concerned. Yet a slight consideration of the subject ought to convince them of their error. If I exchange a horse for a house, it is because the latter is worth more to me than the horse, else why would I make the exchange? And why would the other party exchange if he were not to be a gainer by the transaction? Of course, in this statement, it is implied that both parties have perfect freedom to do as they like. If they are compelled to make exchanges, that is another thing. But if a person is compelled to pay a dollar for a loaf of bread or starve, although by waiting a little time he could get it for one-twentieth of the sum, the case is not changed. One may pay a dollar for a loaf in order to keep from starving, a most exorbitant price perhaps, yet the bread is worth more than the dollar, else it would not be given.

We must not leave out of sight the fact that mankind are continually taking advantage of the situation of things, thus reducing the benefits of exchange to one party and increasing them to the other. As a general rule each party seeks to get the best of a bargain ; that is, to make the most out of it, leaving the least to the other party. Nevertheless, something is always left to both parties. In every contract there is a margin of profits lying between the parties desirous of making it. This profit-margin is of greater or less width. The question with each party is, how much of that margin can I get? If one attempts to get all, the other will not enter into the agreement; a portion must always be left for both. How much can I get and leave enough to the other party to induce him to make and execute the agreement? this is the question which people generally put to themselves when making contracts. Neither party can take all, else the agreement will not be consummated; the profits must be divided between both, and that man is regarded as the most adroit who, by deception and covering up of his situation, by boldness or other means, succeeds in getting the largest portion of that margin and the execution of the agreement. Yet the truth remains, that in every exchange all parties to it are gainers.

Freedom of exchange is affected in three ways: by necessity, by nature, and by law.

By necessity, we mean when men are in such a situation that no option is left them in making an exchange, and they are obliged to pay whatever is asked for a thing. This point we have previously considered, yet we further remark, that the taking advantage of the situation of a person to get an unreasonable price for a thing is to be condemned. If a man is starving, the baker cannot morally ask any more for his bread, although his customer may be abundantly able to pay an increased price; if there is a famine, the price of corn ought not to be enhanced, except so far as may be necessary to lead people into the practice of necessary economy; if money is scarce, the lender ought not to increase rates.

A fair profit is all that a man can morally demand for his wares or services under the usual conditions of society.

Restriction of freedom by nature is when checks to exchange arise from distance, and the like. Thus, wheat we will say is worth seventy-five cents per bushel in New York, and half that sum in Chicago. If it costs thirty cents to transport a bushel of wheat to New York, the cost of transportation is a natural check to the exchange of the grain between the two points. These restrictions of nature often operate as a protection to trade between various sections. Thus, if iron be worth ten cents a pound in New York, and eight in London, and it costs three cents a pound to transport it to New York, none will come hither because the cost of transportation will operate as a protection to the home manufacturer. Such protection, being natural, forms no ground of just complaint.

The freedom of exchange is sometimes interfered with by law. Laws are passed restricting it upon the ground that it is desirable to encourage production at home. A manufacturer says: "B ought not to be permitted to buy his clothes in London, because, though the price may be less, he ought to be willing to pay me more for them in order to encourage home industry and make our country independent of ENGLAND." And if he has not sufficient regard for the good of his country to buy at home, then the manufacturer demands the enactment of a law which shall virtually prevent him from buying abroad and shut him up to the home market.

Many objections have been made to the enactment of protective laws; among others, that the State had no authority to enact them, that it was entirely beyond its power to fetter freedom of trade, and that every individual has the right to buy where he can buy cheapest. Whether this ground be valid depends, as we have previously shown, upon the question, whether it is for the good of the people to enact such laws? if they are to be benefited, no objection can be raised to their enactment. Whether they are to be beneficial or not turns mainly upon the question, will there be less likelihood of other nations making a monopoly of their products if we do not engage in their manufacture? Thus, if we did not manufacture cotton goods, would ENGLAND charge more for them than now? If ENGLAND sells everything to us without reference to production here, there is nothing to the protectionists' claim. If English prices are less than they would have been had ENGLAND remained the sole manufacturer, we are benefited by encouraging home manufactures by application of law.

ENGLAND undoubtedly charges less for many things because we manufacture them. Considering the infirmities of human nature, the desire to take all the advantage of each other we can, we believe that if American industries had not been protected by law, ENGLAND would have proved just as grasping and selfish as other nations, and charged us more than we are now paying for many of the necessities of life.

There is, however, another side to the picture. The principal object of protective laws has been, not to benefit the many, but to enrich the few. There is no virtue, therefore, in that system which has been fostered by legislation. If our manufacturers have increased, and we are made independent of ENGLAND, the object of the Government is pure enough; yet the object of many a manufacturer will not bear examination. Most of them are like the rest of the world, seeking aid from the Government whenever they can, in order to make money.

What conclusion, then, shall be drawn in respect to protective legislation? We cannot reach such a sweeping conclusion as is deduced generally, that protective laws are wholly good or wholly bad. In some instances, undeniably, the building up of our industries at home has made us independent of foreign nations, and we purchase at less prices because we can supply our wants from a wider number of producers. Had we pursued the opposite policy, we should have been screwed down to higher prices. Protection, therefore, in some cases, has been a positive benefit. In the encouragement of the manufacture of cotton and woolen goods we believe that we are the gainers by the system adopted. Were we dependent upon foreign markets, they would charge more. Yet, we must not leave out of sight the fact that ENGLAND, FRANCE, and GERMANY, have been competitors for our trade, and as long as we have such a wide field in which to purchase, there is less danger of being ruled by monopolies.

Protection may be justified upon the ground of preventing a monopoly. Protection is not the proper name to give to such legislation, however. The aim of it is to prevent the commission of a wrong; if it does not effect this purpose, there is no justification for it. England has been able to undersell and monopolize by screwing down the price of labor. Surely it is just to enact a law, if possible, by which labor can get its fair pay.

There is another side to this question and a most important one. We have shown that people are benefited by making exchanges. This is just as true of people living in different countries as in different towns. As between people living in the same town perfect freedom of exchange is not denied. But why should it be denied as between people living in different countries? The answer usually given is, that it is desirable to make every country independent. This we deny. It is not desirable to make any country independent except so far as may be necessary to place it upon an equality with others in making exchanges, in other words, to prevent the operation of monopolies.

The spirit to prevent free intercourse between different countries and to create, if possible, an unnatural advantage of one nation over another is precisely the same spirit which individuals exhibit in their intercourse with each other. Each tries to get the best of the bargain. This is because each is selfish. The same principle crops out in legislation between the various States by which each State tries to get advantages over the rest.

Lastly, it is applied in our intercourse with foreign nations. Protection, therefore, is a radically selfish policy. It is a development of individual selfishness into national selfishness. It is the same old spirit, springing from the same source and incapable of being defended. Of course, if a nation pursues a selfish policy towards us, we must in some way seek to correct it. But we have taken the initiative. We have been selfish when other nations have not. There is no more reason for conducting ourselves differently towards the people of other nations than towards one another, so long as they manifest a right disposition with us. "Hath not GOD made of one blood all nations of men?" And shall we bid eternal defiance to His law, and cultivate selfishness instead of benevolence in our conduct towards one another and towards other nations? Away with such horrible thoughts! let us seek to buy and sell at fair prices, and if we are contented with these, no one will ever hear of a protective policy adopted unless it be to prevent a monopoly.

There has been a great deal of discussion as to whether labor is benefited by protective laws or not. In ENGLAND, the question has been renewed of enacting protective laws for the benefit of the workman. Whether such laws are beneficial to him or not, depends upon the question whether the products of his labor are all sold in his own country or not. If he makes for a foreign market, he wants no protective laws; if he makes for a home market, the fewer foreign products coming into competition with his labor the better for him.

"Does protection protect?" is another question which has given rise to much dispute. The subject is befogged with a great deal of error, and yet it seems to us that the explanation is easy enough. If a duty is laid upon a foreign article so high that it is not imported and the thing is made at home and sold for a profit, there is no question but that protection protects. This is as clear as noonday.

It is unquestionably true that our tariff laws, to a great extent, have operated to shut out foreign goods and encourage home manufactures. But another principle comes in to modify their action. If the iron manufacturer sells his goods at a higher price because the foreign article is shut out, although as low perhaps as he can afford to make it, the parties buying the goods increase the price of their own wares. This is illustrated on a grand scale by the railroad companies. It costs them much more to equip their roads in consequence of the advance in the price of iron, and so they make up the difference by increasing the price of freights. Whether protection protects or not, depends upon the question how generally other persons besides those protected increase the price of their products. If every one increases the price of his products comparatively to the increased cost of iron, all the benefits of protection are lost. All turns upon that. For the protected to get protection, he must not only sell at the higher rate, but others must not change their rates. If they do, he gains nothing in the end.

As a fact in our history, when a tariff has been increased other things have risen in price, one after another, until the rise became so general that the protective effect of the law was gone, resort was then had to additional legislation and the tariff increased once more. Such is a history of tariff legislation in this country. It will be seen, too, the fewer the things protected, the more effectual the law. ' Prices will not rise so rapidly. But if the principle of protection be admitted at all, its logical application spreads over all things, coming in competition with foreign articles. The principle is so well understood now that it is useless to attempt to get more protection; the most that can be hoped is to keep the laws where they are. The last time it was attempted to increase the rates, the bill was defeated on this very ground, that as so many wanted protection the law would be of no avail to any person.

The prime object in establishing protective laws is to benefit a class at the expense of the rest. The intent to benefit the State is always a secondary object in enacting them. The real object is to benefit a few. It is class, not general legislation, and generally has wrought most pernicious effects upon every country indulging in it. If an English manufacturer should cripple an American manufacturer by underselling him in order to break down his business, in such a case the Government could very properly interfere, because it is an attempt to take an undue advantage of another. We have proved that it is the duty of the Government to prevent monopolies and undue advantages. The State can protect its industries, although detrimental for a season to the people, if the object be to build them up and prevent other nations from dictating the price of the commodities protected; that is the sole ground for interfering with freedom of trade. When foreigners seek no such advantage, but sell for a reasonable price, and for less than we can make and sell the same product, it is for our advantage to buy of them, and any interference with that liberty for the sake of benefiting a class is iniquitous.

If it be admitted that protective legislation is for the good of society, of course, it is justifiable. The history of it shows that such is not the fact. It is not the intent of those who specially seek for it, to benefit society so much in general, as themselves in particular. These laws have not had a good effect upon mankind. They have put off the day of universal love and peace, and have glorified the narrowness and littleness of the past. With the narrow, selfish feeling growing out of this policy, upon which in fact it was founded, we have no sympathy. We do not believe in the independence of nations. Dependence upon one another as individuals and nations strengthens the spirit of unity and the bonds of peace. Protection weakens that spirit and encourages war, the greatest scourge of mankind. Conceived in the spirit of personal advantage, the history of protective legislation is one of the saddest which can be read, for it reveals the dreadful selfishness and tyranny of mankind.

There is one other principle pertaining to this subject, that it is not always desirable to be independent of other nations if we could be. We ought not to seek to live within our shell like a turtle. A man who lives only for himself is selfish, runs a miserable life which miserably ends in complete and absolute failure. This is equally true of a nation. If it seeks to live by itself, independent of the rest of the world, having no commerce, no intercourse, it becomes a cold, selfish nation. Its policy is too narrow.

If we can study the design of Providence, He made of one blood all nations of men, and intended that they should dwell together in harmony and unity. He never intended that they should be completely isolated any more than the members of a family. A common life runs through all, and a policy which seeks to destroy that life is contrary to the design of GOD and the best interests of humanity. We were created dependent upon one another, and it is this dependence which makes us sympathetic, peaceful, and eager to help one another. To become independent means to become proud, cold, selfish. This should never be. We can never afford to be independent of other nations, we need their civilization and they need ours.

What a vast benefit commerce has been to the world; but commerce is wholly opposed to the protective policy. How it is breaking down jealousy and enmity between nations! how it is drawing the nations together and working for universal peace! It is linking the whole world in one great brotherhood and putting off forever the day of war and bloodshed. Shall the design of GOD be infringed upon? Shall the world's peace be destroyed? No, never. So long as we have voice or pen it shall support that policy which, we believe, originated in heaven, which tends to destroy human selfishness and pride, which brings the nations of the earth together and makes them one.

Let us revert to the principle with which we set out, that as in individual, so in national exchanges, they are made because both sides must gain. What a grand discovery! "It created a revolution in public opinion and in national policy, which directly affects the happiness of every human being, and forever removed a perennial source of war from the world."

We do not propose to set aside that beautiful truth. We shall recognize it and enforce it, that the selfishness of men may diminish and their good increase.

XVI.

TAXATION.

Taxation is one of the most important functions of Government. The four cardinal rules to be observed in assessing and collecting taxes laid down by ADAM SMITH, have become classic from their frequent repetition, and we cannot do better than state them here.

" 1.—The subject of every State ought to contribute to the support of the Government, as nearly as possible in proportion to their respective abilities; that is, in proportion to the revenue which they respectively enjoy under the protection of the State. In the observation or neglect of this maxim consists what is called quality or inequality of taxation.

" 2.—The tax which each individual is bound to pay ought to be certain, and not arbitrary. The time of payment, the manner of payment, the quantity to be paid, ought all to be clear and plain to the contributor, and to every other person.

" 3.—Every tax ought to be levied at the time, or in the manner in which it is most likely to be convenient for the contributor to pay it.

" 4.—Every tax ought to be so contrived as both to take out and keep out of the pockets of the people as little as possible over and above what it brings into the public treasury of the State."

It was following a natural order to place the rule relating to equality of taxation first, because it is preëminent in importance. We need repeat no commonplaces upon the necessity of observing the rule; the necessity is deeply graven in the popular mind, and no words can deepen or widen that feeling. What we propose to consider are the glaring violations of this rule.

Double taxation is unequal taxation. From this conclusion there is no escape. If A pays a tax upon a piece of property once, and B pays a tax upon a similar piece twice, the latter is doubly and unjustly taxed. No matter in what form the tax is laid, if the specific kind of property is taxed twice it is doubly and wrongfully taxed. Most shocking instances of double taxation have been reported.

The most common method of taxing property twice is in assessing bonds, notes, and other evidences of property. We will begin with the taxation of currency.*

The currency of the country consists principally of the circulation of the National banks which is taxed by the National Government. After such a tax is laid, a subsequent taxing of it in the form of money at interest operates, in most cases, as double taxation. The first tax upon the circulation is well enough, but that ought to be the end of taxing this form of property, as we shall proceed to show.

Smith, the inevitable illustration, has $ 100,000 of this currency. He loans $ 50,000 to Jones, secured by mortgage upon his real estate which is taxed for its full value. Its worth, we will say, is $ 75,000. Two-thirds of it is owned virtually by Smith, and one-third by Jones. But Smith must pay a tax upon his $ 50,000 at interest, and Jones pays a tax upon $ 75,000 of real estate.

* See very interesting article in *Overland Monthly*, vol. ii, p. 351, entitled "Must, Can and Should Money be Taxed?"

Is not this double taxation? Is not JONES taxed upon what he does not actually own to the extent of $50,000?

How, then, shall these two parties be taxed? JONES for the full value of the real estate; for we believe that taxes should be laid upon property rather than upon individuals, because there is a greater certainty in collecting them. Any person who is in possession of property, and is the nominal owner, ought to be taxed for it; and if he is not the actual owner for any or only a part, then he can adjust the payment of the tax with the real parties in interest. This is by far the preferable rule, for it will avoid a vast amount of deception, and the State will collect a larger and juster revenue.

In accordance with this rule, JONES should pay a tax upon $75,000. Being obliged to pay it, he will not give SMITH so much for the use of his money, or he will divide the tax with him according to some agreement made between themselves.

If JONES pays a tax upon that sum, the State ought not to tax Smith for $50,000 loaned to JONES, because it is represented by real estate. It is there. SMITH has transferred it to JONES, who is taxed for it in the form of real estate. SMITH, we will assume, was taxed for it before he loaned the money to JONES, as cash on hand. He lets JONES have it, who puts it into his list. Is it not clear, therefore, to tax SMITH for what he has parted with, for what JONES is taxed, is double taxation? The bank issuing the $100,000 of notes which SMITH has, was taxed for them. SMITH was taxed for them, so long as they were his; when he let JONES have them, the latter was taxed upon his real estate which he received in exchange, and that is a sufficient taxing of all parties.

Let us follow the other $50,000 of SMITH's currency. He loans

$25,000 of it to BROWN, who is a merchant. He expends the money in the purchase of goods. He is taxed for the full value of them. Is there any justice in taxing SMITH for the money loaned to B? Certainly not; it is double taxation.

Smith loans $25,000 to KING, a manufacturer, who expends it in the purchase of cotton for his mill, for wages, or keeps it as cash on hand. In the first case, KING pays a tax upon his raw stock; if he has expended it for wages, he pays a tax on his manufactured product unsold; or, in the third place, he is taxed upon his cash. In either of these three cases, if SMITH pays a tax besides, the same property is taxed twice. If KING has not put SMITH's money into stock, nor manufactured goods on hand, nor has it as cash in the drawer or bank, either he has purchased other property upon which he pays a tax, or he has loaned it to some one else who pays a tax thereon, or he has wasted or lost it in his business. If KING has re-invested it, and pays a tax upon such an investment, there is no justice in taxing SMITH for the same property. If KING has loaned it to another who pays a tax thereon, that is the same thing; if KING has lost or squandered it, surely neither he nor SMITH should pay a tax for what neither one has.

All money is loaned in these ways. We believe these instances cover nearly all cases. It is clear, therefore, that there is no justice in taxing currency after it has been taxed once.

Another way of stating the same conclusion is this: As all indebtedness is equal to the money loaned, the taxation of more than either indebtedness or money is double taxation. The State is constantly transgressing this line, taxing both.

The taxation of bonds falls in the same category as mortgages, except municipal bonds. They represent, in every instance, real or personal property upon which taxes are paid. A railroad corporation, for example, is taxed for all its property. Where is the justice in taxing its bonds? Such bonds are similar to individual mortgages, which we have seen ought not to be taxed.*

It may be said, this question is one purely of the proper assessment of the tax; instead of having A pay upon the property taxed, we require payment to be made of B. True, this is one of the questions involved, and it is a most important one. We insist that only actual, tangible property, and franchises should be taxed, in the possession of the holder if he has a nominal interest therein, although he may not be the actual holder. This rule has the best of reasons to support it. First, it will avoid double taxation. There is no danger of taxing a piece of land twice through mistake. It is sometimes done, but done openly, knowingly. Secondly, it will prevent the commission of fraud. Now, the owners of bonds, notes, and the like do an enormous amount of lying in denying their ownership of such property. Only a very small amount of such property is taxed. Probably not one-twentieth of the bonds in the UNITED STATES which are taxable are put into the lists. People lie and deceive, or in some way evade paying taxes upon them. If actual property were taxed, instead of the evidences of it, there would be no chance of practicing deception. Real estate, goods, and merchandise cannot be put out of existence by words. They exist. How much better, therefore, to tax them, and thus prevent the lying and deception which is universally practiced under the system now prevailing!*

---

* For illustration of the failure to assess and collect taxes upon personal property see Reports of Commissioners to Revise the Laws for the Assessment and Collection of Taxes in the State of New York. 1871-2.

"It has been made manifest to every revenue board that convened at Harrisburg, from February, 1845, to the present time, that the returns of personalty, and, especially, of moneys at interest and stocks, were never a tenth of their actual amounts or values." Report of Commissioners to City of Philadelphia to Revise the Laws Relating to Taxation. P. 9.

Suppose this simple rule were adopted, how far and wide-reaching it would be! It would cover all mortgages and bonds except those issued by municipalities. It would cover all stocks except those of money associations, which should be taxed upon their franchises—a thing that cannot be lost out of sight by words. It would cover all money at interest, inasmuch as this is loaned to persons who have invested it in goods and the like, upon which a tax is paid. The only species of property not covered by the rule is simply the money which a person may have on hand; and as this cannot be in value above the whole amount of currency issued upon which a tax has been paid by the banks issuing it, there is no reason for taxing it a second time.

Were this principle of taxing property adopted, it would be more just than any other, because the tax would be paid where protection to the property is rendered. The ground for taxing property is protection given; but what protection does the State of NEW YORK, for instance, exercise over property situated in MASSACHUSETTS? A lives in Albany, and he holds a mortgage upon a piece of property located in the latter State. A tax is paid upon the property by B. The property is protected by MASSACHUSETTS. True A and B are the owners, but the property is not in Albany, hence it ought not to be taxed there. If A's deed were stolen, the State of NEW YORK might assist him in punishing the offender, but the property, of which the deed is merely the evidence, is in MASSACHUSETTS, is protected by the laws there, and A is indebted to that State, not NEW YORK, for the protection of his property. The same is true of railroad bonds and stocks. There is no justice in taxing the evidence of property in a place away from where it is, because no protection is given.

It will be said that if the evidences of property are not taxed, great hardship may arise. The following case may be supposed. A man lives in Boston owning one hundred thousand dollars of New York Central Railroad bonds. He pays no taxes where he lives, but enjoys all the privileges of the city and educates his children at the public expense. It is asked, is this right? To this question two answers may be given. First, his bonds are the memoranda of property existing in New York, where he must pay a tax to benefit other people and educate their children. Secondly, every individual pays a personal tax for the benefits accruing to the person, and this should cover a tax to support public education.

A lives in Boston, but owns a farm in WISCONSIN, where it is taxed. All admit that this tax is correctly laid. A owns bonds or stock in a WISCONSIN railroad, which are taxed there, and yet he has to pay another tax upon his stock or bonds in Boston. Is not the latter tax as unjust as if his farm in WISCONSIN were also taxed at his place of residence?

Were this rule adopted, of taxing visible, actual property, and franchises, all property would be taxed and more equally than now. Our present mode is barbarous in the extreme, leading to a vast deal of deception and lying, and enabling thousands who ought to pay taxes to escape with paying none. This subject merits the serious attention of economists and legislators, and provision ought to be inserted in every constitution prohibiting double taxation. For this end all should work, for with this to rest upon the present absurd and unjust system of taxation generally prevailing throughout our country can be broken down, and another formed, having its origin in equity and justice.

www.ingramcontent.com/pod-product-compliance
Lightning Source LLC
Chambersburg PA
CBHW020823230426
43666CB00007B/1074